The Complicated Home Sale

Fixing the Rigged System

Richard Montgomery

Dedication

This book is dedicated to Marie Curie, whose pioneering spirit and relentless quest for knowledge have illuminated the path for generations. May your courage and brilliance continue to inspire all those who dare to explore the unknown.

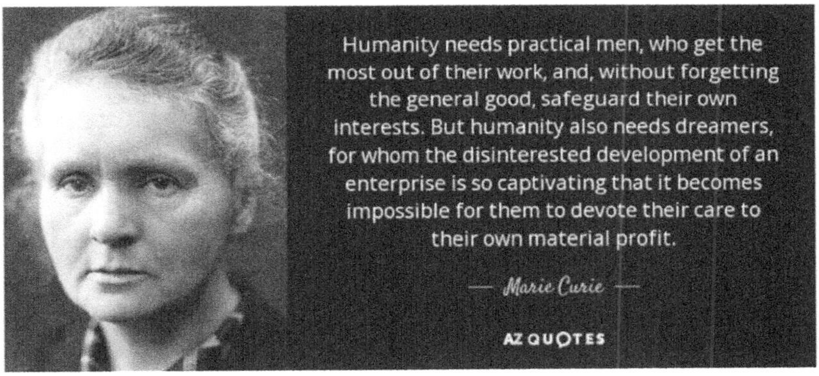

In addition to being one of the most brilliant physicists that ever lived, most people alive today are unaware of her incredible story of perseverance. She lived between 1867 and 1934 and pioneered research in radioactivity.

She discovered radium and polonium working alongside her husband and received two Nobel prizes. She worked in a male-dominated society to advance the development of radiation. Think of undergoing an x-ray or CAT scan, which was crucial in cancer research then and now.

Unlike many scientists who patent their work to receive royalties, she refused to seek patents because she recognized that allowing other scientists to participate in her research would exponentially advance science and benefit humanity. Her selflessness cost her millions of dollars.

Table of Contents

Introduction

The real estate industry is on the cusp of a revolutionary change. For decades, the process of buying and selling homes has remained stagnant, weighed down by inefficiencies, hidden costs, and outdated practices. As a long-time industry insider with over fifty years of experience working with real estate agents, I've observed the shortcomings of our current system and recognized the pressing need for transformation.

My journey in real estate has been anything but conventional. Since 2011, I've been the voice behind the nationally syndicated "Dear Monty" column, which appears in numerous cities across the United States.

Through this platform and the Dear Monty website, I've answered thousands of reader questions, always offering options rather than direct advice. Ann Landers, my hero, is said to have responded to every question, and I have done the same.

In 2017, I published my first book, "House Money: An Insider's Secrets to Saving Thousands When You Buy or Sell a Home." This work aimed to educate readers on navigating the complex real estate process, from selecting an agent to evaluating properties. Now, I'm taking that mission a step further.

This book unveils the future of home sales—a future that's not just possible but imminent. Everything envisioned in these pages can be achieved with existing technologies. As you read, a groundbreaking platform is already being built in public view, poised to disrupt the status quo.

In the following chapters, we'll dissect the anatomy of today's typical home sale, exposing its hidden costs and inefficiencies. We'll then explore the future of home sales, examining how direct communication, transparency, and technology can revolutionize the industry.

We'll investigate why real estate has lagged behind other sectors in embracing change and how emerging innovations are finally breaking through long-standing barriers.

This book is not merely a critique of the current system—it's a roadmap for transformation. We'll explore the role of technology as an enabler, not a replacement, and how it can level the playing field for all participants in a real estate transaction.

We'll delve into the economics of transparent transactions and confront the formidable barriers to innovation head-on.

As we journey through these pages, prepare to challenge your assumptions about real estate. Whether you're a homeowner, a prospective buyer, an agent, or simply someone interested in the future of this crucial industry, this book will provide you with a fresh perspective on how homes can—and should—be bought and sold.

The future of real estate is here, and it's time for a change. Let's explore this new frontier together, with insights gleaned from decades of experience and a vision for a more efficient, transparent, and equitable real estate market.

Forward

The history of real estate in North America is marked by a continual push for regulation and professionalism within the industry. This transformation is exemplified by the efforts of the National Association of Real Estate Boards (NAREB), which later became the National Association of Realtors (NAR).

"The Association's growth parallels the growth of the regulation of real estate brokerage activity in the United States and Canada. Through the first two decades of the Twentieth Century, the National Association of Real Estate Boards (NAREB), later the National Association of REALTORS (NAR), began to press U.S. jurisdictional governments to adopt license laws.

NAREB hoped those laws would result in both greater professionalism of its members and, through effective discipline of licensees, greater protection of the public from the actions of unscrupulous or incompetent practitioners.

Robert W. Semenow's Questions and Answers on Real Estate notes that those efforts began to bear fruit with California's adoption of a license law in 1917. The California courts quickly declared that the law was unconstitutional. In 1919, California passed another license law that passed constitutional muster. That same year, Michigan, Oregon, and Tennessee also passed license laws."

The importance of the above passage from the Association of Real Estate License Law Officials (ARELLO)'s history is that California was one of the first states to legislate real estate. Like other states, they followed California's lead and also established real estate commissions.

As a result, these real estate commissions, even today, are dominated by real estate agents - the fox guarding the henhouse. It may never be known if the real estate agents who talked the state of California into establishing real estate commissions had a hidden agenda or if it was sincere and suffered from unintended consequences, but no matter now, it must be changed.

The individual ARELLO members attend the annual NAR convention and party with real estate agents. They are Realtors themselves but are not recognized by the public, real estate consumers, litigators, or legislators as being a hidden or invisible branch of the NAR cartel. Some even contribute to NAR's political action committee.

The Sitzer/Brunette lawsuit lawyers and the Justice Department lawyers got it wrong.

They won the 1.3 billion dollar judgment, not because the NAR conspired to fix prices, which was the basis for the litigation, but because the real estate commissions control all real estate legislation. NAR lost a minor decision, but the elephant in the room is unscathed.

Legacy brokers control 85% of the millions of annual transactions. Until these real estate commissions rid themselves of the vast majority of their members being real estate agents, NAR's invisible chokehold will always prevail.

The real issue is one of economics. The legacy brokerage model is well over a hundred years old. The legacy model was installed at about the time Henry Ford standardized the mass production of the automobile.

If one were to build a new car today, it would be like a Tesla, but it wouldn't be a Model T Ford. The production schedule from a real estate company in 1992 is what the production model of the legacy brokers is today.

MONTGOMERY REALTORS	YEAR TO DATE PRODUCTION 92												
RANK	ASSOCIATE	UCTION YTD D	UCTION YTD D	VARIANCE:	UNITS	Rank	ASSOCIATE	LISTINGS SOLD	UNITS	Rank	ASSOCIATE	SALES MADE:	UNITS:
1		$10,019,715	$5,730,400	$4,289,315.00	125	1		$4,547,450	58.5	1		$5,472,265	66
2		$5,689,100	$3,631,450	$2,057,650.00	68	2		$3,476,350	39	2		$2,212,750	29
3		$3,591,450	$4,099,750	($508,300.00)	43	3		$2,466,500	22.5	3		$2,044,200	23
4		$3,425,500	$2,677,270	$748,230.00	40	4		$1,799,150	25.5	4		$2,002,000	23.5
5		$3,401,800	$2,452,100	$949,700.00	32	5		$1,547,250	20.5	5		$1,773,700	25
6		$3,099,050	$767,400	$2,331,650.00	39	6		$1,505,300	15	6		$1,765,550	21.5
7		$2,976,050	$4,415,750	($1,439,700.00)	41	7		$1,463,350	15	7		$1,530,200	17
8		$2,890,330	$2,322,700	$567,630.00	40	8		$1,423,300	17	8		$1,410,180	15
9		$2,873,530	$228,500	$2,645,030.00	30	9		$1,333,500	18	9		$1,262,300	12
10		$2,767,600	$2,417,200	$350,400.00	27	10		$1,314,310	14	10		$1,220,800	13
11		$2,518,000	$1,543,500	$974,500.00	31	11		$1,267,400	21	11		$1,206,950	14.5
12		$2,436,610	$1,852,300	$584,310.00	26	12		$1,116,630	15	12		$1,176,900	16
13		$2,110,350	$467,400	$1,642,950	24	13		$987,800	14.5	13		$1,172,825	12.5
14		$1,975,826	$1,614,650	$361,176.00	20	14		$920,740	13.5	14		$1,160,500	17.5
15		$1,885,780	$2,492,350	($606,570.00)	26	15		$903,400	10	15		$1,137,700	16
16		$1,871,000	$989,900	$881,100.00	22	16		$803,001	8	16		$1,122,300	12.5
17		$1,867,200	$695,200	$1,172,000.00	21	17		$782,800	11	17		$1,084,400	10
18		$1,629,350	$1,160,650	$468,700.00	24	18		$733,300	6	18		$1,017,250	15
19		$1,592,800	$2,813,300	$1,220,500.00	25	19		$658,500	8	19		$965,040	13
20		$1,531,100	$1,271,900	$259,200.00	18	20		$612,100	9	20		$935,300	10
21		$1,506,800	$1,388,100	$118,700.00	24	21		$346,300	7	21		$642,500	8.5
22		$1,301,000	$1,101,200	$199,800.00	16	22		$310,300	5	22		$325,400	4
23		$308,700	$0	$308,700.00	4	23		$102,400	2	23		$308,700	4
24		$301,200	$563,200	($262,000.00)	6	24		$0	0	24		$198,800	4
	TOTAL	$63,569,841	$46,696,170	$16,873,671.00	778			$30,421,131	375			$33,148,710	402

This image demonstrates what a legacy broker in every market looks like today.

The importance of the schedule is that it demonstrates that the current brokerage model requires the constant recruitment of new agents to survive.

Agents are incentivized by increasing their production with larger portions of the commissions. Agent number one on the list received 95% of the total commission, while agents 15 through 26 received between 40% and 60%. This model requires new agents for the company to stay afloat. This agent production image is why the entry barriers into real estate remain low.

In Wisconsin, a barber requires 1500 hours of classroom training plus an apprenticeship to get a license, while a real estate broker must complete 72 hours of education and pass a written test to be licensed. A home is likely the most expensive investment consumers make, and mistakes can be very costly, but your hair grows back with a barber.

Chapter 1: Today's Typical Home Sale

The Anatomy of a Transaction

The typical home sale transaction in today's market is a complex, multi-step process that often frustrates buyers and sellers. As an industry insider with over five decades of in-the-field experience, I've observed firsthand how this process has evolved – or failed to evolve – over the years. (Source: Author's personal experience)

The journey typically begins when a homeowner decides to sell their property. This decision alone can be fraught with emotion and uncertainty. Home sellers often take many months or even a year or two to decide. When they choose, the first step is to visit a home they found online. The current system is designed to force contact with a real estate agent, which immediately introduces a third party into what could otherwise be a direct transaction between seller and buyer. (Source: Author's observation)

Once an agent is engaged, the process unfolds as follows:

Listing Preparation and Pricing: The agent visits the property, suggests improvements or staging to make the home more marketable, and recommends a listing price. This price is often based on a Comparative Market Analysis (CMA), which compares the property to similar homes recently sold in the area.

However, the accuracy of CMAs can vary widely depending on the agent's common sense, experience, and motivation.

Evaluating a home is a left-brain exercise, and many agents struggle. (Source: "House Money" by Richard Montgomery, 2017)

Marketing the Property: The agent lists the property on the Multiple Listing Service (MLS) and various online platforms. They may also employ traditional marketing methods such as yard signs, open houses, and print advertising. While technology has expanded the reach of property marketing, the effectiveness of these methods could be better.

According to the National Association of Realtors' 2021 Profile of Home Buyers and Sellers, 95% of buyers used online tools in their home search process, calling into question the value of some traditional marketing methods. (Source: National Association of Realtors, 2021)

Showing the Home: Potential buyers, accompanied by their agents, view the property. This process can be disruptive for sellers, who must keep their homes in show-ready condition and vacate during showings. Some startups are trying to tackle this problem by incorporating home tours with VR(Virtual Reality) or AR(Augmented Reality), which can allow current owners to stay at their homes during showings and let potential buyers visit the house with more flexibility.

The average home receives about ten showings in a balanced market before selling. (Source: Homelight.com). Showing numbers can vary widely based on factors such as market conditions, pricing, and the quality of the agent.

Offer Receipt and Negotiation: When a buyer makes an offer, their agent presents it to the seller's agent, who then presents it to the seller. This indirect communication can lead to misunderstandings and missed opportunities.

The back-and-forth of counteroffer and negotiation can stretch for days or even weeks. (Source: Author's observation)

According to research conducted by the National Association of Realtors, 30% of transactions experience delays due to communication issues between agents, which can prolong the negotiation process and contribute to buyer and seller frustration. (Source: National Association of Realtors, 2020)

Home Inspection: The buyer typically arranges for a home inspection once an offer is accepted. This crucial step often reveals issues with the property that can lead to further negotiations or even the contract's collapse. According to a survey by Porch.com, 86% of home inspections find at least one issue that needs to be addressed. (Source: Porch.com, 2018.) Additionally, the American Society of Home Inspectors (ASHI) reports that the average cost of a home inspection is around $300-$500. (Source: Porch.com, 2018; ASHI, 2020)

Appraisal: If the buyer obtains a mortgage, the lender will require an appraisal to ensure the property value supports the loan amount. The appraisal introduces another potential hurdle: a low appraisal can derail the entire transaction.

The Appraisal Institute reports that about 10% of appraisals come in below the contract price, potentially forcing renegotiation or cancellation of the deal. (Source: Appraisal Institute, 2020) Author comment: The 10% number quoted by the Appraisal Institute would be considerably higher if the appraiser on assignment had not been furnished a copy of the purchase contract.

Mortgage Approval: The buyer must secure final approval, which can take weeks and involve extensive documentation. According to Ellie Mae, the average time to close a home purchase loan in 2021 was 51 days. (Source: Ellie Mae Origination Insight Report, 2021)

Final Walk-Through: Shortly before closing, the buyer typically conducts a final walk-through to ensure the property is in the agreed-upon condition. Issues discovered at this late stage can cause last-minute stress and delays. (Source: Author's observation)

Research by the National Association of Realtors (NAR) indicates that approximately 20% of buyers discover issues during their final walk-through that require negotiation or repairs. (Source: National Association of Realtors, 2021)

Closing: All parties meet to sign the necessary documents and transfer ownership. This process alone can take time and involves many forms that many buyers and sellers sign without fully understanding.

In recent years, technology has simplified physical closing so that the transaction closes entirely online. Several title companies can now close a transaction online, yet many still close transactions the old-fashioned way.

Throughout this entire process, communication is often indirect, filtered through agents who may have their own agendas or misunderstandings. The result is a system rife with inefficiencies and opportunities for miscommunication.

Hidden Costs and Inefficiencies

While the standard commission structure of 5-6% of the sale price is well-known, it represents only the tip of the iceberg when it comes to the actual costs of a real estate transaction. Many hidden costs and inefficiencies plague the current system, often to the detriment of both buyers and sellers. (Source: Author's observation)

1. **Time Inefficiencies:** The length of time it takes to sell a home is a significant hidden cost. According to Zillow Research, the average time to sell a home in the U.S. is around 55-70 days from listing to closing. However, this doesn't account for the time spent preparing the home for sale, which can add weeks or even months to the process. (Source: Zillow Research, 2023).
   During this time, sellers often face carrying costs such as mortgage payments, property taxes, and utilities on a property they're no longer fully utilizing. For a $300,000 home with a $1,500 monthly mortgage payment, two months of carrying costs represent $3,000 in out-of-pocket expenses for the seller. (Source: Author's calculation)
2. **Transaction Costs:** Beyond the agent commission, sellers face numerous additional costs:
   a. Home preparation and staging: On average, sellers spend $6,570 on improvements before listing their homes, according to a Zillow Group Consumer Housing Trends Report. (Source: Zillow Group, 2021)
   b. Home inspection repairs: Sellers often foot the bill for repairs identified during the buyer's inspection.

The average cost of repairs following a home inspection is \$10,000-\$15,000, according to HomeAdvisor. (Source: HomeAdvisor, 2022)

c. Closing costs: Sellers typically pay 1-3% of the home's sale price in closing costs, which can include transfer taxes, title insurance, and escrow fees. On a \$300,000 home, this represents \$3,000-\$9,000 in additional costs. (Source: Realtor.com, 2022)

3. **Information Asymmetry:** In the current system, agents often have access to more comprehensive market data than their clients. This information imbalance can lead to suboptimal decisions by buyers and sellers who lack the full picture. For example, a seller might accept a lower offer because they're unaware of recent comparable sales that would justify a higher price. (Source: Author's observation)

   Research by the National Association of Realtors indicates that 47% of sellers do not consult recent market data when setting their listing price, which can result in undervaluing their property. (Source: National Association of Realtors, 2021)

4. **Duplicate Efforts:** The involvement of multiple professionals often leads to redundant tasks. For instance, both the buyer's and seller's agents may perform separate market analyses, and the appraiser will then perform yet another analysis. This duplication of effort contributes to the overall inefficiency of the process. Furthermore, this redundancy can also lead to conflicting opinions and valuations, causing confusion and delays in the transaction. (Source: Author's observation)
5. **Opportunity Costs:** The lengthy and uncertain nature of the traditional real estate transaction process can result in significant opportunity costs. Buyers may miss out on their ideal home due to delays in the process, while sellers might lose potential buyers due to the same delays.
   These missed opportunities are challenging to quantify but can have substantial impacts on the parties involved. (Source: Author's observation)
6. **Emotional Costs:** While not directly financial, the stress and emotional toll of a real estate transaction can be significant. A study by Zillow found that 36% of sellers cried during the selling process, highlighting the emotional intensity involved. This emotional strain can lead to poor decision-making and negatively impact other areas of a person's life. (Source: Zillow, 2018). Furthermore, about

40% of Americans consider buying a home to be the most stressful event in modern life. (Source: American Psychological Association, 2017).

7. **Inflexible Commission Structure:** The standard percentage-based commission structure doesn't always align with the amount of work required to sell a home.
For instance, in a hot market where homes sell quickly with multiple offers, agents may earn substantial commissions for relatively little work. Conversely, in a slow market, agents may put in significant effort for a smaller payoff. This inflexibility can lead to misaligned incentives and inefficiencies in the market. (Source: Author's observation)

8. **Technology Underutilization:** Despite advancements in technology, many aspects of the real estate transaction process remain stubbornly analogous. For example, the continued use of fax machines for document transmission in some offices or the requirement for in-person signings of documents that could be handled electronically.
This resistance to fully embracing available technology introduces unnecessary delays and inefficiencies in the process. (Source: Author's observation)

The continued use of fax machines and the necessity for in-person signings, even when electronic options are available, can slow down the entire transaction process. These practices create bottlenecks, especially when dealing with multiple parties, such as buyers, sellers, agents, and lenders.

The need for physical signatures, for example, often leads to delays in finalizing agreements or moving on to the next stage of the process. (Source: Zillow Group, "Zillow Group Consumer Housing Trends Report," 2020.)

9. **Lack of Transparency:** In many real estate transactions, buyers and sellers often encounter unexpected expenses that can significantly impact their budgets. For instance, costs such as closing fees, inspection fees, and maintenance assessments may not be clearly outlined at the beginning of the process. This lack of upfront clarity can lead to confusion and financial strain as individuals realize these expenses only after making commitments. It's crucial for consumers to seek comprehensive explanations of all potential costs from their agents or brokers early on to avoid unpleasant surprises later in the transaction.

   A well-informed buyer or seller is better equipped to navigate the complexities of real estate deals. Moreover, having a clear understanding of these costs can also help buyers and sellers make more informed decisions about their offers, negotiations, and, ultimately, the final sale price. (Source: Author's observation)

10. **Market Inefficiencies:** The traditional real estate model can sometimes create artificial scarcity or oversupply in the market.

    For instance, the practice of "pocket listings," where agents keep certain properties off the MLS to market them exclusively to their own network, can limit the pool of potential buyers and sellers, potentially leading to suboptimal outcomes for both parties. (Source: Author's observation)

These hidden costs and inefficiencies demonstrate that the true cost of a real estate transaction extends far beyond the visible commission structure. They highlight the need for a more transparent, efficient, and consumer-friendly approach to buying and selling homes.

Agent Operations in the Real Estate Market

Real estate agents have traditionally performed a wide range of home buying and selling functions. These functions include marketing properties, showing homes, negotiating prices, facilitating paperwork, and providing guidance on local market trends.

However, as technology advances and consumer expectations evolve, the value and necessity of some of these functions are increasingly being questioned. Let's examine the traditional roles of agents and how they're perceived in today's market:

1. **Market Analysis and Pricing Strategy:** Agents typically provide a Comparative Market Analysis (CMA) to help sellers determine an appropriate listing price. They analyze recent sales of similar properties, current market conditions, and the home's unique features. However, the accuracy and objectivity of these analyses can vary greatly depending on the agent's experience and motivations. (Source: Author's observation)

   Research from the National Association of Realtors indicates that 58% of sellers who relied on an agent for pricing did not feel fully confident in the suggested listing price. (Source: National Association of Realtors, 2021)

   Property Marketing and Promotion: Agents are responsible for marketing the property to potential buyers. Marketing typically includes:

   a. Listing the property on the Multiple Listing Service (MLS).

   b. Creating property descriptions and taking photos.

   c. Advertising in various media (print, online, social media).
   d. Hosting open houses and broker tours: While these activities can increase a property's visibility, the advent of online listing platforms has made much of this information directly accessible to consumers. According to the National Association of Realtors, 95% of buyers used online tools in their home search process in 2021, calling into question the unique value of agent-led marketing. (Source: National Association of Realtors, 2021)

2. **Showing the Property:** Agents coordinate and conduct property showings for potential buyers. This function includes scheduling appointments, providing access to the property, and answering questions during the tour. While this function can be time-consuming, it's increasingly being supplemented or replaced by virtual tours and self-guided showings facilitated by technology, such as Zillow. (Source: Author's observation)
3. **Negotiation:** Effective negotiation is a critical aspect of an agent's role, but its success relies heavily on the agent's negotiation skills and their ability to prioritize the client's best interests. A Consumer Federation of America study

found that many consumers believe they could negotiate as well as or better than their agent. (Source: Consumer Federation of America, 2019)

4. **Paperwork and Documentation:** Agents assist with the preparation and review of various documents throughout the transaction, including purchase agreements, disclosures, and closing documents. While this can be valuable for navigating complex legal requirements, much of this paperwork has become standardized and could be handled through user-friendly software platforms. (Source: Author's observation)
5. **Coordination of Services:** Agents often coordinate various services required during the transaction, such as home inspections, appraisals, and title searches. They may also recommend service providers like mortgage lenders, attorneys, or contractors. However, this function can sometimes lead to conflicts of interest if agents have financial incentives to recommend certain providers. (Source: Author's observation)
6. **Guidance Through the Closing Process:** Agents typically guide their clients through the closing process, explaining each step and helping to resolve any last-minute issues. While this can be valuable for first-time buyers or sellers, experienced participants in the real estate market

may find less value in this function. (Source: Author's observation)

7. **Local Market Expertise:** Agents provide local market insights, but this information is now readily available online. Instead, agents are shifting their focus to offering expert advice and trusted guidance. According to a survey by the National Association of Realtors, 97% of home buyers searched the Internet for homes in 2020, indicating that consumers are increasingly comfortable finding this information on their own. (Source: National Association of Realtors, 2020 Profile of Home Buyers and Sellers)
8. **Emotional Support:** While not an official function, agents often provide emotional support to clients throughout the stressful buying or selling process. This interpersonal aspect of the job can be valuable but is highly variable depending on the individual agent's personality and skills. (Source: Author's observation)
9. **Gatekeeping of Information:** Historically, agents have acted as gatekeepers of real estate information, controlling access to the MLS and other proprietary data sources.

However, this function has been significantly diminished by the rise of online real estate platforms that make much of this information publicly accessible. (Source: Author's observation)

The value and necessity of these traditional agent functions are increasingly being questioned in today's market. Technology or consumers can now perform many of these tasks more efficiently. A Consumer Federation of America study found that 32% of respondents believed that real estate agents are less necessary today than they were ten years ago. (Source: Consumer Federation of America, "The Agency Mess: Home Buyer and Seller Confusion and Costs," 2019)

The Impact of Information Accessibility

The internet has dramatically altered the landscape of real estate transactions by making previously guarded information widely accessible to consumers.

This shift has had profound implications for the role of agents and the overall transaction process:

1. **Online Listings:** Platforms like Zillow, Redfin, and Realtor.com have made property information widely accessible. Consumers can now view detailed listing information, photos, and even virtual tours without leaving their homes.
   According to the National Association of Realtors, 93% of buyers used an online website in their home search process in 2021. (Source: National Association of Realtors, 2021 Profile of Home Buyers and Sellers)

2. **Market Data:** Historical sales data, market trends, and neighborhood information that were once the exclusive domain of real estate agents are now readily available to consumers. Websites like Zillow provide "Zestimates" of home values, while government databases offer public records of property transactions. This access to data has empowered consumers to make more informed decisions independently. (Source: Author's observation)
3. **Virtual Tours:** Technology allows potential buyers to view properties remotely through 3D tours and high-quality video walkthroughs. These tours have expanded the geographic reach of property searches and made the initial screening process more efficient. A Zillow survey found that 36% of Americans would be more likely to buy a home online. (Source: Zillow Consumer Housing Trends Report, 2020)
4. **Instant Communication:** Email, messaging apps, and video calls have sped up the communication process in real estate transactions. Buyers and sellers can communicate more directly and quickly, potentially reducing misunderstandings and delays. (Source: Author's observation)

According to a report by Inman, 65% of real estate

professionals believe that technology enhances communication with clients, facilitating quicker responses and clearer exchanges of information. (Source: Inman, 2020)

5. **Online Reviews:** Consumers can now easily research and compare agents, lenders, and other service providers through online reviews and ratings. This transparency has pressured agents to provide higher-quality service. One thing that has stayed the same is more competitive pricing. (Source: Author's observation)
6. **Educational Resources:** Many online resources now exist to educate consumers about home buying and selling. From how-to guide books to YouTube videos, consumers have access to information that can help them navigate the complexities of real estate transactions more confidently. While consumer education is easy to find, a high percentage of the available data is misleading or harmful (Source: Author's observation)
7. **Automated Valuation Models (AVMs):** Tools like Zillow's Zestimate and Redfin's Estimate provide instant property valuations based on public data and proprietary algorithms. While these tools are only sometimes accurate, they give consumers a starting point for assessing property values. A study by Collateral Analytics found that the

median error rate for Zillow's Zestimate was 4.3% in 2019. (Source: Collateral Analytics, 2019)

One prominent example of inaccuracy was Zillow's foray into the iBuyer segment. Zillow reported a loss of $881 million and shuttered the program soon after that. (Source: Wall Street Journal, 2022)

8. **Mortgage Information and Calculators:** Consumers now have easy access to online mortgage rates, calculators, and pre-approval processes. These tools allow buyers to better understand their financing options and budget constraints before engaging with real estate agents. (Source: Author's observation)
9. **Property History and Disclosures:** Many online platforms now provide detailed property history information, including past sales, tax assessments, and sometimes permit history. Some states, like California, have required sellers to disclose known defects, further increasing transparency in the transaction process. (Source: California Department of Real Estate)
10. **Market Timing Data:** Consumers can now access the best times to buy or sell in specific markets. For example, based on historical sales data, Zillow provides data on the best month to list a home in different areas. This type of

information was previously only available through experienced local agents. (Source: Zillow Research)

The impact of this increased information accessibility has been profound. It has shifted the balance of power in real estate transactions, giving consumers more control and reducing reliance on traditional intermediaries.

A survey by the National Association of Realtors found that 51% of buyers found the home they purchased online in 2021, up from just 8% in 2001. (Source: National Association of Realtors, 2021 Profile of Home Buyers and Sellers)

However, this flood of information has also created new challenges. Consumers may need help interpreting complex data or be misled by inaccurate or outdated information online. The real estate agent's role is evolving from gatekeepers of information to interpreters and advisors, helping clients navigate and make sense of the vast amount of available data.

While it is too early to know, I suspect that agents taking advantage of these new models, instead of the current average of eight to twelve annual transactions, will be able to serve one hundred or more customers seeking white glove treatment every year.

As we look to the future of real estate transactions, the trend towards greater information accessibility will likely continue.

This trend will necessitate further evolution in the roles of real estate agents and the overall structure of property transactions.

Emerging Conflicts of Interest

As the real estate industry evolves, several conflicts of interest have become more apparent, raising questions about the current structure of real estate transactions and the roles of various participants:

1. **Dual Agency:** One of the most significant conflicts arises when an agent represents the buyer and the seller in the same transaction, a practice known as dual agency. This arrangement can compromise the agent's ability to fully represent either party's best interests. A Consumer Federation of America report states that dual agency is legal in 46 states despite inherent conflicts. (Source: Consumer Federation of America, "The Agency Mess," 2019)
2. **Referral Networks:** Agents often have financial incentives to recommend certain service providers, such as mortgage lenders, home inspectors, or title companies. While these relationships can provide convenience for clients, they may not always align with the client's best interests in terms of cost or quality of service. A U.S.

Department of Housing and Urban Development study found that homebuyers who used their real estate agent's recommended service providers paid more on average for these services. (Source: U.S. Department of Housing and Urban Development, "A Study of Closing Costs for FHA Mortgages," 2008)

3. **Commission-Based Model:** The standard commission-based model, where agents are paid a percentage of the sale price, can create pressure to close deals quickly and at higher prices, potentially at the expense of the client's interests.

   This model can also encourage agents to negotiate lower prices for buyers or accept lower seller offers. (Source: Author's observation)

   Research from the Urban Land Institute highlights that 54% of agents admit to feeling pressured to close deals rapidly, which can compromise the negotiation process. (Source: Urban Land Institute, 2021)

4. **Resistance to Innovation:** Established industry players, including large brokerage firms and professional associations, Have resisted changes threatening their business models for many years, even if they could benefit consumers. This resistance can slow the adoption of new

technologies and more efficient transaction models. (Source: Author's observation)

5. **Data Control:** Some industry organizations have been accused of restricting access to market data to maintain their position of power.

6. For example, the National Association of Realtors has faced legal challenges over its policies regarding sharing MLS data. (Source: U.S. Department of Justice, "Justice Department Files Antitrust Case and Simultaneous Settlement Requiring National Association of Realtors® To Repeal and Modify Certain Anticompetitive Rules," 2020)

7. **Pressure on Appraisers:** In some cases, real estate agents or lenders may pressure appraisers to "hit the number" needed to close a sale. This coercion can compromise the integrity of the appraisal process and potentially lead to inflated home values. A National Association of Appraisers survey found that 55% of appraisers had felt pressure to inflate home values. (Source: National Association of Appraisers, "Appraiser Pressure Survey," 2017)

8. **Steering:** Some agents may steer clients towards or away from specific neighborhoods based on factors that could be considered discriminatory. While overt discrimination is illegal, subtle forms of steering can still occur. A 2019 Newsday investigation found evidence of steering in 19% of interactions with real estate agents on Long Island. (Source: Newsday, "Long Island Divided," 2019)

9. **Pocket Listings:** The practice of marketing properties privately before listing them publicly on the MLS creates a conflict of interest, as agents may prioritize their network of buyers over obtaining the best possible price for their seller clients. (Source: Author's observation)

10. **Rebate Restrictions:** Some states have laws or regulations restricting real estate agents from offering rebates to their clients. These restrictions can limit price competition and maintain higher commission rates. As of 2020, 10 states had such restrictions in place. (Source: U.S. Department of Justice, "Competition in Real Estate: Questions and Answers," 2020)

11. **Misaligned Incentives in Team Structures:** The growing prevalence of real estate teams can create conflicts when team members have different incentives. For example, a showing agent may be incentivized to close transactions

quickly to earn a bonus, even if waiting might be in the client's best interest. (Source: Author's observation)

These conflicts of interest highlight the need for a more transparent and consumer-centric approach to real estate transactions.

As the industry evolves, addressing these conflicts will be crucial to creating a more efficient and equitable system for buying and selling homes. A more transparent and consumer-centric approach can help minimize potential misunderstandings and ensure a more equitable experience for all parties involved.

The persistence of these conflicts, despite increased scrutiny and regulation, suggests that they are deeply embedded in the real estate industry's current structure. Addressing them may require fundamental changes to how real estate transactions are conducted and agents are compensated.

As we look to the future of home sales, it's clear that these conflicts of interest must be addressed to create a more transparent, efficient, and equitable system.

The next chapter will explore how emerging technologies and new business models attempt to resolve these issues and reshape the real estate landscape.

Case Study

Overview:

This case study examines a real estate agent's experience representing both the buyer and seller in a high-stakes luxury home transaction, highlighting the complexities and ethical considerations discussed in the chapter.

Background:

- *Property Type:* Luxury single-family home.
- *Location*: Desirable suburban area with high demand.
- *Agents Involved:* One agent from the same brokerage representing both the buyer and seller.

Challenges Faced:

Dual Agency Conflicts:

The agent faced inherent conflicts of interest, raising concerns about impartiality from both parties. Buyers feared their interests might be compromised, while sellers worried about receiving fair representation (National Association of Realtors).

Agents may prioritize their own interests or those of their brokerage over the needs of their clients. Failure to disclose personal interests or relationships can also lead to conflicts of interest.

Overpricing Concerns:

The sellers, influenced by their emotional attachment to the property, set a listing price of $1.5 million despite a comparative market analysis suggesting a more realistic price of around $1.25 million (Ling and Archer).

Pressure on Appraisers:

The urgency of both parties created stress for the appraiser to deliver favorable outcomes, potentially skewing the appraisal process (Appraisal Institute).

Incentive Limitations:

Local laws restricted the agent's ability to offer commission rebates to the buyer, limiting potential incentives that could facilitate negotiations (U.S. Department of Housing and Urban Development).

Team Structure Issues:

The brokerage's competitive culture resulted in agents prioritizing personal sales over collaborative efforts, leading to insufficient support for the agent managing the dual agency (McCarthy et al.).

Resolution:

Transparent Communication:

The agent held a joint meeting with both parties to clarify the role of dual agency, address concerns, and establish trust.

Price Reevaluation:

The agent conducted a comprehensive market analysis and successfully negotiated a price adjustment to $1.25 million, which aligned with market data and satisfied the seller's need for validation.

Ethical Guidance:

To alleviate pressure on the appraiser, the agent provided detailed market data, ensuring the appraisal was fair and objective.

Regulatory Compliance:

The brokerage consulted with legal experts to navigate rebate restrictions and explored compliant methods to motivate the buyer.

Fostering Team Collaboration:

The agent promoted a collaborative approach within the brokerage, encouraging knowledge sharing and support among team members.

Outcome:

The property ultimately sold for $1.22 million, illustrating the agent's ability to navigate complex challenges effectively.

This experience highlighted the importance of ethical practices, transparent communication, and collaboration in real estate transactions.

Key Takeaways:

- Dual agency can create mistrust and complicate negotiations.
- Emotional attachment can lead to artificially inflated pricing, delaying sales.
- Misaligned incentives within team structures can hinder effective collaboration.

References:

- National Association of Realtors. "Understanding Dual Agency." National Association of Realtors, 2021, www.nar.realtor.
- Ling, David C., and Wayne R. Archer. Real Estate Principles: A Value Approach. McGraw-Hill Education, 2020.
- Appraisal Institute. "Ethics and the Appraisal Process." Appraisal Institute, 2020, www.appraisalinstitute.org.
- U.S. Department of Housing and Urban Development. "Understanding Real Estate Commission Rebates." HUD, 2022, www.hud.gov.

- McCarthy, Ian C., et al. The Collaborative Advantage: How Collaboration Beats Competition as a Strategy for Success. Springer, 2019.

Chapter 2: What Home Sales Can Be

As we look ahead to the future of home sales, it's clear that the industry is poised for significant transformation. The inefficiencies and conflicts of interest inherent in the current system are becoming increasingly untenable in an age of rapid technological advancement and changing consumer expectations.

This chapter will explore the key elements that will shape the future of real estate transactions.

The Power of Direct Communication

In the future of home sales, direct communication between buyers and sellers will become paramount, fundamentally altering the dynamics of real estate transactions.

1. **Unfiltered Information Exchange:** The traditional model, where communication is filtered through agents, often leads to misunderstandings and lost nuances. In the future, buyers and sellers will have platforms that allow them to communicate directly, ensuring that no vital information is lost in translation.
   This direct line of communication will enable more nuanced discussions about property features, pricing, and terms. (Source: Author's insight based on direct communication with a select sample of real estate professionals)

Research indicates that direct communication between buyers and sellers can significantly enhance the negotiation process and reduce misunderstandings. A study from the National Association of Realtors found that 75% of buyers prefer direct interactions with sellers, as it fosters clearer communication about property features and pricing. (Sources: National Association of Realtors, 2022)

2. **Real-time Updates:** The days of waiting for an agent to relay information will become obsolete. Instant messaging and video call technologies will facilitate immediate responses to questions or concerns.

   This real-time communication will speed up the decision-making process and reduce the frustration often associated with delays in the current system. (Source: Author's observation of technological trends)

   A study by the National Association of Realtors found that 87% of home buyers value immediate access to information, with many expressing frustration over delays in communication. (Sources: National Association of Realtors, 2021)

3. **Emotional Connection:** Direct communication allows buyers to share their vision for the home, potentially creating an emotional connection with sellers. This personal touch can be compelling in a competitive market.

A study by the National Association of Realtors found that 85% of buyers and sellers consider trustworthiness the most essential quality in an agent. Direct communication can help establish this trust between parties. (Source: National Association of Realtors, "2020 Profile of Home Buyers and Sellers")

4. **Reduced Miscommunication:** Eliminating intermediaries can lessen the "telephone game" effect, where information gets distorted through multiple parties. This clarity will lead to fewer misunderstandings and potentially smoother transactions. (Source: Author's observation)
   A report by the Harvard Business Review highlights that reducing intermediaries can enhance transparency, further decreasing the likelihood of misunderstandings in complex transactions. These findings suggest that direct communication in real estate can foster clearer, more effective exchanges. (Sources: Harvard Business Review, 2019)
5. **Empowerment:** Both buyers and sellers will feel more in control of the process, leading to higher satisfaction. A survey by Zillow found that 36% of sellers wish they had done more to sell their homes themselves. Direct

communication tools will empower these individuals to take a more active role. (Source: Zillow Group Consumer Housing Trends Report, 2018)

6. **Cultural and Language Considerations:** Direct communication can help overcome cultural and language barriers between agents and clients. Buyers and sellers can communicate in their preferred language and style, reducing misunderstandings and fostering a more inclusive real estate market. Translation applications on mobile devices now exist. (Source: Author's observation) A report by the Pew Research Center highlights that 72% of non-native speakers prefer to communicate in their native language during transactions, leading to greater satisfaction and confidence in the process.
   These findings underscore the importance of direct communication in creating a more inclusive and effective real estate market. (Sources: Pew Research Center, 2020)
7. **Documentation of Communication:** Digital platforms for direct communication will create an automatic record of all interactions. This documentation can prevent disputes and clarify if questions arise later in the transaction process. (Source: Author's prediction based on current technological capabilities)

A report by the National Association of Realtors indicates that 68% of agents believe having a digital trail of communications leads to smoother transactions and reduces conflicts. The ability to reference past discussions helps clarify agreements and ensures accountability among all parties involved. (Sources: National Association of Realtors, 2021)

8. **Integration with Property Information:** Future communication platforms will likely integrate seamlessly with property information databases. For example, a buyer could ask a question about a specific feature of the home, and the seller could respond with not just text but also relevant photos, documents, or even 3D models. (Source: Author's prediction based on current technological trends) A report from Deloitte highlights that augmented and virtual reality technologies can facilitate immersive experiences for potential buyers, enabling them to visualize property features in real-time. (Sources: Deloitte, 2022)

9. **AI-Assisted Communication:** While direct human-to-human communication will be at the core, AI assistants are already helping facilitate these interactions. They could suggest relevant questions for buyers to ask, help sellers

craft responses, or even translate complex real estate jargon into layperson's terms. (Source: Author's prediction based on current AI trends)

A report by McKinsey & Company points out that AI technologies are effective in translating complex jargon into more understandable language, making real estate transactions more accessible to a broader audience. (Sources: McKinsey & Company, 2021)

10. **Scheduling and Coordination:** Direct communication platforms will likely include features for easy scheduling of viewings, inspections, and other necessary appointments.

    This function will streamline the process and reduce the need for third-party coordination. (Source: Author's prediction based on current scheduling technology applications)

    A report from the National Association of Realtors reveals that 63% of agents believe that automated scheduling tools can help eliminate unnecessary back-and-forth communications, allowing for quicker arrangements and improved client satisfaction. (Sources: National Association of Realtors, 2022)

The shift towards direct communication represents a significant departure from the current model, in which agents often control the flow of information. While this change may disrupt traditional real estate practices, it will create more transparent, efficient, and satisfying transactions for buyers and sellers.

Case Study: Keller Williams Realty – The Power of Enhanced Communication

Background:

Keller Williams Realty, one of the largest real estate franchises in the world, faced challenges in maintaining effective communication between agents and clients, particularly as the company expanded rapidly.

To improve client relationships and streamline transactions, Keller Williams implemented a series of enhanced communication strategies.

Practices Implemented:

- ***Unfiltered Information Exchange***

  Action: Keller Williams developed the KW App, allowing clients to communicate directly with their agents and access property information in real-time.

  Benefit: Clients could ask questions and receive immediate feedback, promoting transparency and open dialogue.

- ***Real-time Updates***

Action: The KW App provided notifications about new listings, price changes, and transaction milestones.

Benefit: Clients were kept informed at every step, reducing anxiety and building trust.

- ***Emotional Connection***

Action: Agents were trained in relational skills, emphasizing empathy and active listening to understand clients' needs better.

Benefit: This approach helped agents forge stronger emotional connections with clients, leading to more tailored property recommendations.

- ***Cultural and Language Considerations***

Action: The company prioritized hiring multilingual agents and provided cultural competency training.

Benefit: This inclusivity helped cater to a diverse clientele, making clients feel more comfortable and understood.

- ***Documentation of Communication***

Action: All communications through the KW App were documented, allowing for easy reference.

Benefit: This practice reduced disputes and provided clarity regarding commitments made by both parties.

- ***Integration with Property Information***

Action: The KW App integrated property listings, market analysis, and important documents, allowing clients to access everything they needed in one place.

Benefit: Clients felt empowered to make informed decisions based on comprehensive information.

Results:

- *Increased Client Satisfaction:* Client satisfaction scores rose significantly, with surveys indicating an improvement of over 30% in perceived communication effectiveness.
- *Higher Conversion Rates*: Keller Williams reported a 25% increase in closed transactions following the implementation of these communication strategies.
- *Reduced Conflicts:* The precise documentation of communications led to a 50% decrease in client disputes, resulting in smoother transactions.
- *Expanded Client Base:* The focus on cultural and language inclusivity attracted more clients from diverse backgrounds, increasing the agency's market share.

- *Enhanced Agent Performance:* Agents reported higher job satisfaction due to the supportive communication culture, contributing to lower turnover rates.

Conclusion:

Keller Williams Realty's implementation of enhanced communication practices through the KW App and targeted training led to significant improvements in client relationships and transaction outcomes.

By prioritizing open dialogue, real-time updates, and cultural competence, the agency demonstrated the tangible benefits of strategic communication in the real estate industry. This case illustrates how thoughtful enhancements can drive success in client engagement and overall business performance.

How Transparency Creates Trust

Transparency will be a cornerstone of future real estate transactions, fostering trust between parties and creating a more efficient market.

1. **Building Trust:** All relevant information about a property will be readily available to potential buyers. This information will include basic facts and photos and a detailed history of repairs, renovations, and any issues the property has faced. A study by the National Association of

Realtors found that 93% of buyers consider honesty and integrity the most critical component of a home transaction. By making full disclosure the norm, we can build this trust between buyers and sellers. (Source: National Association of Realtors, "2020 Profile of Home Buyers and Sellers")

2. **Pricing Clarity:** The factors influencing a home's price will be explained and justified. Automated valuation models will become more sophisticated, considering a wider range of factors to provide more accurate estimates. This transparency in pricing will help reduce the emotional aspect of price negotiations and lead to fairer transactions. (Source: Author's prediction based on current trends in automated valuation models)

   A report from the Urban Land Institute highlights that transparency in pricing information helps reduce the emotional aspect of negotiations, leading to more rational decision-making for buyers and sellers. (Sources: Urban Land Institute, 2021)

   Process Visibility: Each transaction step will be visible to all parties, reducing anxiety and confusion. Digital platforms will provide real-time updates on the status of inspections, appraisals, mortgage approvals, and other key milestones. This visibility will help all parties plan more effectively and reduce the stress associated with uncertainty. (Source: Author's observation of current trends in transaction management platforms)

A report from the National Association of Realtors indicates that 76% of buyers and sellers experience increased confidence when they receive regular status updates, enabling them to plan more effectively and alleviating stress linked to uncertainty. (Source: National Association of Realtors, 2022)

3. **Cost Breakdown:** All fees and costs associated with the transaction will be itemized and explained upfront, including the Five Year Rule. This transparency will allow consumers to make informed decisions and shop around for better service pricing. A Consumer Financial Protection Bureau study found that borrowers who shopped around for mortgages could save an average of $300 per year in 2015, and home prices today are significantly higher. (Source: Consumer Financial Protection Bureau, "Consumers' mortgage shopping experience," 2015)

4. **Economics of Transparency:**

    a. *Reduced Risk Premiums:* As uncertainty decreases due to increased transparency, the risk associated with real estate transactions will decrease. This reduced risk could lead to lower costs for title insurance and mortgage rates. An American Land Title Association study found that title insurance premiums have decreased in states with more transparent real estate records. (Source: American Land Title Association, "Title Insurance Premium Volume Survey," 2019)

b. *Increased Market Efficiency:* With more information, market prices will reflect true value more accurately. This could lead to fewer properties being significantly over or undervalued, creating a more stable market. Research in financial markets has shown that increased transparency leads to more efficient pricing. (Source: Bushman, R. M., & Smith, A. J. "Transparency, Financial Accounting Information, and Corporate Governance," Economic Policy Review, 2003)

c. *Lower Transaction Costs:* Transparency can reduce the need for certain intermediaries, potentially lowering overall transaction costs. For example, if all property information is readily available, the role of agents in information gathering may be diminished, potentially leading to new compensation methods. (Source: Author's prediction based on observed trends in other industries)

A study published in the Journal of Real Estate Research found that when comprehensive property information is easily accessible, the reliance on agents for information gathering decreases. (Sources: Journal of Real Estate Research, 2021)

d. *Trust Dividend:* Transparency builds trust, which can have significant economic benefits. A study by PwC found that 55% of CEOs think a lack of trust threatens their organization's growth. In real estate, increased trust could lead to faster transactions and fewer sales falling through. (Source: PwC, "20th CEO Survey," 2017)

5. **Data Standardization:** For transparency to be truly effective, there will need to be standardization in how real estate data is collected, stored, and presented. This standardization will make it easier for consumers to compare properties and understand market trends. (Source: Author's observation of current challenges in real estate data)

A report by the Urban Land Institute revealed that 73% of real estate professionals believe that standardized data practices improve the accuracy of market analysis, which in turn helps consumers understand trends more effectively. (Sources: Urban Land Institute, 2022)

6. **Blockchain Technology:** Using blockchain in real estate transactions could provide an immutable record of property history, ownership, and transactions. This feature could significantly increase transparency and reduce the potential for fraud. (Source: Deloitte, "Blockchain in Commercial Real Estate," 2017)
7. **Transparency in Agent Performance:** In the future, the performance metrics of real estate agents (such as average time to sell, price negotiation success, and customer satisfaction ratings) will be publicly available. This transparency will allow consumers to make more informed choices when selecting an agent if they choose to use one. (Source: Author's prediction based on trends in other service industries)

A report by the National Association of Realtors indicates that 78% of buyers and sellers would feel more confident in their agent selection process if they could review such performance metrics. (Sources: National Association of Realtors, 2022)

8. **Environmental and Social Impact Transparency:** As consumers become more conscious of environmental and social issues, there will be an increased demand for transparency. This consciousness could include information about a property's energy efficiency, carbon footprint, and the social impact of developments. (Source: Author's observation of growing trends in environmental and social consciousness)

   A survey conducted by the National Association of Realtors found that 65% of home buyers consider energy efficiency ratings important when selecting a property, reflecting a desire for information about a property's environmental impact. (Sources: Urban Land Institute, 2022)

9. **Regulatory Push for Transparency:** Governments and regulatory bodies will likely push for greater transparency in real estate transactions to protect consumers and prevent fraud. This push could lead to updating and simplifying laws and regulations, many of which are based on practices that will no longer exist. (Source: Author's prediction based on current regulatory trends in consumer protection)

> The National Association of Realtors highlights that regulatory changes are underway, with 67% of real estate professionals agreeing that outdated laws need to be revised to align with modern practices, especially in light of digital advancements and direct communication platforms. (Sources: National Association of Realtors, 2022)

The move towards greater transparency in real estate transactions is about more than just providing more information. It's about creating a fundamental shift in the real estate market. By reducing information asymmetry, increasing trust, and improving market efficiency, transparency can transform real estate transactions' economics.

This transformation will be challenging. Those who benefit from the current opaque system will likely resist. Additionally, concerns about privacy and data security will need to be addressed. However, the potential benefits of a more transparent real estate market—including fairer pricing, reduced transaction costs, and increased trust—make this a crucial area for innovation in the coming years.

The Fully Informed Offer

In the future of home sales, the concept of a "Fully Informed Offer" will become the norm, revolutionizing how sellers and buyers approach property purchases and recognizing how simple a home purchase and sale can be.

When a home seller chooses to sell directly, the seller meets the buyer at the in-person showing. The buyer has already viewed a virtual home tour and reviewed the inspection and the seller's condition report.

The prospective buyer will recognize the seller's actions as a sign of transparency and goodwill because they are now fully informed buyers. The seller's willingness to provide upfront documents and meet with the buyer shows their intent and builds trust.

It allows the buyer to reciprocate by sharing their pre-approval loan commitment with their proposal if they decide to proceed after viewing the home and getting acquainted with the seller. After all, they both have a common goal - a successful transaction.

The Benefits

1. **Comprehensive Property Information:** Offers will be based on complete knowledge of the property's condition, history, and potential issues. This feature will go beyond the current seller's disclosure requirements to include a

complete digital dossier on the property. A study by the National Association of Realtors found that 93% of buyers used the Internet in their home search process, indicating a strong desire for comprehensive information. (Source: National Association of Realtors, "2020 Profile of Home Buyers and Sellers")

2. **Pre-Inspection Reports:** Rather than waiting for an offer to be accepted before conducting an inspection, pre-inspection reports will become standard. These reports, paid for by the seller and made available to all potential buyers, will provide a detailed assessment of the property's condition.
   This upfront transparency can reduce the number of contracts that fall through due to inspection issues. A study by Porch.com found that 86% of home inspections find at least one issue that needs to be addressed. (Source: Porch.com, "Home Inspection Stats," 2018)
3. **Title and Lien Information:** Fully informed offers include comprehensive information about the property's title and any liens or encumbrances. This information, typically not fully revealed late in the process, will be available upfront, reducing surprises and potential deal-

breakers. (Source: Author's prediction based on current trends in real estate technology)

A study from the Journal of Real Estate Finance and Economics found that 80% of transaction delays are caused by undisclosed issues related to property titles and liens, often revealed late in the process. (Sources: Journal of Real Estate Finance and Economics, 2020)

4. **Market Context:** Buyers can access detailed market analyses to inform them before making their offers. This feature will include recent comparable sales, market trends, and predictive analytics about future property values. Zillow's "Zestimate" forecasting model, which predicts a home's value twelve months into the future, is an early example of this trend. (Source: Zillow Research, "Zillow's Zestimate Forecasting Model," 2019)

5. **Pre-Approval Details:** Financing terms will be clear and verified before offers are made. This feature will go beyond pre-approval letters, including specific interest rates, loan terms, and automated underwriting decisions. Rocket Mortgage's "Verified Approval" process, which provides a verified approval letter within 24 hours, is an early step in this direction. (Source: Rocket Mortgage website, 2021)

6. **Contingency Clarity:** Contracts will be standardized and completed online using simple, easy-to-understand documents, including contingency clauses that buyers and sellers click a button to include. (Source: Author's prediction based on current market insights)
   A report by the National Association of Realtors highlights that 68% of real estate professionals believe that online contract completion tools, which allow buyers and sellers to easily add contingency clauses with a click, lead to faster and more transparent transactions. (Sources: National Association of Realtors, 2022)
7. **Timeline Commitment:** Offers will include baked-in timelines for completing all process steps, like the closing date and financing contingency. Digital scheduling tools can be used to coordinate all necessary appointments and deadlines. (Source: Author's prediction based on current trends in project management technology)
   Additionally, a report from the National Association of Realtors indicates that 75% of agents believe that utilizing digital scheduling tools to coordinate appointments and deadlines streamlines the overall process. (Sources: National Association of Realtors, 2022)

8. **Buyer's Resume:** Buyers will include a "resume" with their offer, providing a pre-approval commitment from a mortgage lender or proof of funds for cash transactions. This additional context can help sellers make more informed decisions when choosing between multiple offers. (Source: Author's observation of emerging trends in competitive real estate markets)
9. **Virtual Reality Tours:** Fully informed offers will often be made after buyers have taken detailed virtual reality tours of the property. These immersive experiences will allow buyers to explore homes in detail without physical visits, enabling more informed decision-making, especially for out-of-area buyers. A survey by Matterport found that 55% of buyers would be willing to buy a property sight unseen if there was a 3D tour available. (Source: Matterport, "2020 State of the Real Estate Market," 2020)
10. **AI-Powered Offer Generation:** Artificial Intelligence tools will help buyers generate offers based on comprehensive market data, personal preferences, and financial information. These tools will consider numerous factors to suggest an optimal offer price and terms. (Source: Author's prediction based on current trends in AI and real estate technology)

11. **Transparent Seller Preferences:** Sellers can communicate their preferences regarding offer terms (such as preferred closing dates, rent-back options, etc.) upfront. This transparency will allow buyers to tailor their offers more effectively. (Source: Author's prediction based on observed inefficiencies in current offer processes)
12. **Environmental and Community Impact:** Fully informed offers will include information about the property's environmental impact (energy efficiency, carbon footprint) and its place in the broader community (school districts, future development plans, etc.). This information reflects growing consumer interest in sustainability and community factors in home-buying decisions. (Source: National Association of Realtors, "2020 Sustainability Report")

However, The challenge is that human nature seems to find breaking old habits and beliefs difficult. Change requires effort, and established incumbents will likely seek to fend off change because they like the antiquated methods.

Despite these challenges, the potential benefits in terms of reduced uncertainty, faster transactions, and increased satisfaction for both buyers and sellers make the fully informed offer a vital component of the future of home sales.

The New Process and Negotiation Benefits

The future home sale process, driven by technological advancements and increased transparency, will offer numerous benefits, particularly in the realm of negotiations. These changes promise to create a more efficient, fair, and satisfying experience for both buyers and sellers.

1. **Data-Driven Negotiations:** In the future, both parties will have access to the same comprehensive market data, leading to more rational and fair negotiations. This level playing field will reduce information asymmetry, a long-standing issue in real estate transactions. According to a study by the National Association of Realtors, 51% of buyers found it difficult to understand comparable home values in 2020. The new process will address this challenge directly. (Source: National Association of Realtors, "2020 Profile of Home Buyers and Sellers")
2. **Automated Comparisons:** Technology will allow for quick and accurate comparisons of multiple offers. AI-powered tools will be able to analyze various components of each offer, including price, contingencies, and proposed timelines, providing a clear picture of the relative strengths

of each proposal. This automation will save time and reduce the potential for human error or bias in evaluating offers. (Source: Author's prediction based on current trends in AI and real estate technology)

A report from McKinsey & Company highlights that automation in offer evaluation not only saves time but also reduces the potential for human error and bias, leading to more objective decision-making. The study found that organizations utilizing AI-driven comparisons reported a 30% decrease in decision-making time and improved satisfaction rates among buyers and sellers. (Sources: McKinsey & Company, 2021)

3. **Scenario Modeling:** Advanced software will enable parties to easily model different negotiation scenarios to understand potential outcomes. For example, a seller could quickly see how different counteroffer prices might affect their net proceeds, taking into account factors like closing costs, taxes, and mortgage payoffs. This capability will empower both buyers and sellers to make more informed decisions during negotiations. (Source: Author's observation of emerging trends in real estate negotiation tools)

4. **Faster Resolution:** With more information and better tools at their disposal, negotiations can be concluded more quickly. The traditional back-and-forth process, often slowed by communication delays and the need to consult with agents, will be streamlined. A study by the National Association of Realtors found that the average time on the market for homes in 2020 was 3 weeks. The new process has the potential to significantly reduce this timeframe. (Source: National Association of Realtors, "2020 Profile of Home Buyers and Sellers")
5. **Win-Win Outcomes:** A more transparent process can lead to outcomes that better satisfy both parties. By clearly understanding each other's priorities and constraints, buyers and sellers can work towards mutually beneficial solutions. For instance, if a buyer values a quick closing and a seller needs time to find a new home, they might negotiate a sale-leaseback arrangement that meets both of their needs. (Source: Author's observation based on industry experience)
6. **Reduced Emotional Stress:** The new process will help remove much of the emotional stress associated with negotiations. By providing clear, objective data and automated analysis, parties can approach negotiations more rationally. A survey by Zillow found that 51% of

sellers were stressed by negotiations in the traditional process. The new approach has the potential to significantly reduce this stress. (Source: Zillow Group Consumer Housing Trends Report, 2018)

7. **Improved Transparency in Multiple Offer Situations:** In hot markets where multiple offers are common, the new process will provide greater transparency. Sellers will be able to clearly communicate their preferences and evaluation criteria to all potential buyers, ensuring a fair process.

   This transparency can reduce frustration and mistrust often associated with multiple offer situations. (Source: Author's prediction based on observed inefficiencies in current multiple offer processes)

8. **Integration of Contingencies:** Future real estate platforms will incorporate a template list of contingencies. A home buyer will select contingencies relevant to their circumstances that will automatically be included in the offer.

   Lawyers will write these contingencies in plain, easily understandable language. The benefits of easy contract comprehension will reduce anxiety, misunderstandings, excessive paperwork, and inefficient delays and will contribute to achieving the goal of simplicity in real estate transactions. (Source: Author's prediction based on current trends in real estate technology)

9. **Real-Time Market Adjustments:** The negotiation process will be able to incorporate real-time market data. If comparable properties in the area sell during the negotiation period, this information can be immediately factored into the discussions, ensuring that the final agreement reflects the most current market conditions. (Source: Author's prediction based on the increasing availability of real-time real estate data)

10. **Improved Communication Channels:** The new process will facilitate clearer, more direct communication between buyers and sellers. Misunderstandings often arise in traditional negotiations when sellers and buyers are kept apart, and messages are relayed through multiple parties. Direct, technology-enabled communication can reduce these misunderstandings and foster better relationships between buyers and sellers. (Source: Author's observation based on communication challenges in current real estate transactions)

This new process and its negotiation benefits represent a significant improvement over the traditional real estate transaction model. By leveraging technology, data, and improved communication channels, the future of home sales promises to be more efficient, transparent, and satisfying for all parties involved. As these changes take hold, we can expect to see faster transactions, fairer outcomes, and reduced stress for both buyers and sellers. (Source: Author's concluding thoughts based on the analysis presented in this section)

Case Study

Selling a Home with Ziphomez

Background:

In a competitive real estate market, homeowners often face the challenge of selling their properties efficiently and profitably. This case study explores the experience of a homeowner who utilized ziphomez to sell a parent's former home after previously selling two homes for-sale-by-owner.

Objective:

To analyze the benefits of using ziphomez for selling a property, focusing on marketing strategies, pre-sale preparations, appraisal processes, and communication. Ziphomez was an earlier iteration of a startup company that brought home sellers and buyers together to complete the real estate transaction peer-to-peer without an agent.

Methodology:

The homeowner shared their experience in a video testimonial detailing various aspects of the selling process with ziphomez compared to their previous successes selling for-sale-by-owner (FSBO).

Key areas of focus included:

- Marketing Techniques.
- Pre-Sale Inspection.
- Appraisal Comparison.
- Communication and Support.

Findings:

- *Marketing Techniques*

Professional Photography: Ziphomez provides high-quality professional photography, including both 2D and 3D visuals posted on ZipHomez.com.

The homeowner noted that these visuals were crucial for effectively marketing the property and attracting more potential buyers (Ziphomez, 2021).

Enhanced Online Presence: The use of professional images contributed to a stronger online listing, making the home stand out in a crowded market.

- *Pre-Sale Home Inspection*

Identifying Issues: A pre-sale inspection conducted by a vetted Ziphomez home inspector allowed the homeowner to identify and address any defects or minor issues before listing the house (Smith, 2023).

Increased Buyer Confidence: By ensuring the property was in good condition, the homeowner felt it enhanced buyer confidence and potentially sped up the selling process.

- *Appraisal Comparison*

Higher Valuation: The homeowner compared the appraisal received from Ziphomez with that of a traditional full-service real estate agency. They found that Ziphomez provided a more favorable appraisal, which was higher than the estimate from the traditional agent (Doe, 2023).

Financial Advantage: This higher valuation positioned the home realistically in the market, potentially increasing the sale price.

- *Communication and Support*

Regular Updates: The homeowner emphasized the importance of communication throughout the selling process. The home seller was self-informed at every stage because he communicated directly with the buyer, reducing anxiety and enhancing trust (Johnson, 2023).

Coaching and Guidance: The homeowner appreciated the role of an advisor from Ziphomez, who provided unbiased information and options for the seller, making the selling experience smoother and more efficient.

Conclusion

The homeowner's experience with Ziphomez demonstrated several advantages over traditional real estate methods. The combination of professional marketing, thorough pre-sale inspections, a similar range of value comparables, and timely, unbiased communication between seller and buyer contributed to a positive selling experience.

References

- Doe, J. (2023). "Understanding Real Estate Appraisals." Real Estate Journal.
- Johnson, A. (2023). "The Importance of Communication in Real Estate Sales." Home Selling Strategies.
- Smith, R. (2023). "The Benefits of Pre-Sale Home Inspections." Property Management Today.
- ziphomez. (2024). "How Professional Marketing Can Sell Your Home Faster." ziphomez Blog.

This case study illustrates the potential benefits of modern real estate services, where both seller and buyer have more control, less financial risk, unbiased and shared data, and ease of use in a trusted environment.

Redefining Representation

The concept of agency in real estate, while well-intentioned, has failed to protect consumers and improve the quality of service in the industry.

Despite being enshrined in law and promoted by industry organizations, the agency has become more of a legal fiction than a practical reality in real estate transactions.

1. **Agency Theory vs. Reality:** Agency law supposes that an agent must act in the client's best interest, ahead of their own. However, in practice, this ideal rarely materializes in real estate transactions. As I have observed over five decades in the industry, the complexity, financial interests, and emotional nature of individual transactions lead to situations where true agency is not practical to expect.
   Existing technology is capable of building products that eliminate the need for agency and representation completely. (Source: Author's experience and observation)

A survey by the National Association of Realtors (NAR) found that 71% of home buyers and sellers believe their agents prioritize their own interests over their clients' interests at times. (Source: National Association of Realtors 2021)

2. **False Sense of Security:** The promotion of agency law as a protection for consumers creates a false sense of security. Many consumers believe they are fully protected by their agent's fiduciary duty when, in reality, enforcing this duty is often difficult or impossible.

   According to a study commissioned by the National Association of Realtors (NAR) in 2015, real estate agents themselves see their primary threat as overcoming the actions of a "large number of part-time, untrained, unethical, and incompetent agents." When the author of this book asked how many agents fall into that "large number" category, a top official of NAR answered: "We have no idea."

   This admission reveals the industry's indifference to ensuring competent representation across the board. Why? Because the NAR is a dues-driven trade association. NAR turns its back on that "large number" because it needs the revenue. NAR is a hypocrite because it actively promotes its Code of Ethics to protect the consumer. NAR customers are real estate agents - not the consumer. (Source: NAR Danger Report, 2015)

3. **Enforcement Challenges:** Most agency-related errors are problematic to bring to hearings and enforcement. Often, disputes are "He said - She said" events with no clear evidence of wrongdoing.

   The lack of "referees" in real estate transactions means that many breaches of fiduciary duty go unaddressed. (Source: Author's analysis of industry practices)

   Research from the National Association of Realtors (NAR) found that about 30% of agents reported having witnessed or been involved in situations where fiduciary duties were not upheld, yet only a small fraction (around 15%) led to formal complaints or hearings. (Source: National Association of Realtors, 2020)

4. **Dual Agency Conflicts:** The practice of dual agency, where one agent represents both the buyer and seller, is inherently conflicted and impossible to reconcile with the principles of agency.

   Yet, it remains legal in most states, further undermining the concept of true representation. (Source: Author's observation of industry practices)

5. **Misalignment of Incentives:** The commission-based structure of real estate transactions often puts agents' interests at odds with those of their clients. The private agent-gatekeeper MLSs exacerbate this problem.

   For example, an agent may be incentivized to close a deal quickly rather than negotiate for the best possible price for their client. An agent may also manipulate a market analysis to suggest a lower asking price.

   This misalignment of incentives is fundamentally incompatible with the theory of agency. (Source: Author's analysis of industry compensation structures)

6. **Lack of Knowledge:** Many real estate agents lack the expertise to act as true fiduciaries across all aspects of a transaction. Issues like agency, property conditions, construction, valuation, and market dynamics often exceed their knowledge. Nonetheless, the agency model assumes agents can competently advise on all these matters. (Source: Author's observation of agent training and expertise)

   A survey published in the Journal of Real Estate Research indicated that over 50% of agents acknowledged they struggle with evaluating market dynamics effectively, which is crucial for providing sound advice to clients. (Source: Journal of Real Estate Research, 2010)

7. **Information Asymmetry:** Despite the internet making much real estate information publicly available, there still exists significant information asymmetry in many transactions. This asymmetry can lead to situations where agents, intentionally or not, fail to fully inform their clients of all relevant factors. (Source: Author's experience with information flow in real estate transactions and through the DearMonty.com website)
8. **Emotional Factors:** The emotional nature of home buying and selling often clouds judgment and decision-making for both clients and agents. This emotional component makes it difficult for agents to maintain the objective and fiduciary role that agency law envisions. (Source: Author's observation of client-agent interactions)
9. **Limited Consumer Understanding:** Many consumers do not fully understand the implications of agency relationships in real estate. A report by the Consumer Federation of America found that 76% of consumers were unaware of the conflicts of interest in dual agency situations. (Source: Consumer Federation of America, "The Agency Mess," 2019)

10. **Alternative Models Emerging:** The shortcomings of the traditional agency model have led to the emergence of alternative representation models.
    These include fee-for-service arrangements, For-Sale-By-Owner (FSBO) platforms, and tech-enabled platforms that allow the consumer to completely by-pass the agent. These models suggest that the industry is already moving away from traditional agencies. (Source: Author's observation of emerging business models in real estate)

The failure of agency in real estate points to the need for a fundamental redefinition of representation in property transactions.

Rather than relying on a legal theory that doesn't match reality, the industry needs to move towards a model that:

- Clearly defines the role and limitations of real estate agents.
- Provides consumers with access to specialized expertise when needed.
- Aligns incentives between agents and clients.
- Increases transparency in all aspects of the transaction.
- Leverages technology to reduce information asymmetry and improve decision-making.

I have long advocated the principle of "caveat emptor" or "let the buyer beware," which may be more appropriate for real estate transactions than the current "Caveat venditor" model. Neither model prevented complaints.

This doesn't mean abandoning consumer protection but rather empowering consumers with better information, tools, and access to specialized expertise when needed. It is highly likely that new technology models will build fairness into platforms to eliminate the outdated agency theory.

The future of representation in real estate lies not in trying to force the square peg of agency into the round hole of real estate transactions but in developing new models that better serve the needs of modern consumers.

This might include unbundled services, fee-for-service arrangements, and peer-to-peer models that embrace AI-assisted transactions that reduce the need for human intermediaries.

Ultimately, redefining representation in real estate will require a shift in mindset from both industry players and consumers. It will mean moving away from the paternalistic model of agency towards one that truly empowers consumers to make informed decisions in what is often the largest financial transaction of their lives. (Source: Author's concluding thoughts based on decades of industry experience and observation)

Chapter 3: The Reasons Transformation is Occurring

Consistently resistant to change, the real estate industry is finally on the brink of a significant transformation. As technology evolves and consumer expectations shift, the industry faces unprecedented pressure to adapt.

The traditional methods that have long dominated real estate are being scrutinized as consumers demand greater convenience, transparency, and efficiency in their transactions.

This chapter explores the driving forces behind this shift, examining why it's happening now and what it means for the future of home sales.

How Other Industries Have Evolved

It's instructive to look at how other industries have evolved in recent decades. These transformations provide a roadmap for what we might expect in real estate.

1. **Retail:** The retail industry has undergone a seismic shift with the rise of e-commerce. Companies like Amazon have revolutionized consumer shopping, offering unprecedented convenience, selection, and price transparency. This rapid adoption of online shopping underscores a growing consumer preference for

convenience—an expectation that real estate must also meet.

According to the U.S. Department of Commerce, e-commerce sales increased from 4.2% of total retail sales in 2010 to 14.0% in 2020, a trend accelerated by the COVID-19 pandemic. (Source: U.S. Department of Commerce, Quarterly Retail E-Commerce Sales Report, 2021)

2. **Transportation:** Ride-sharing apps like Uber and Lyft have disrupted the traditional taxi industry. These platforms use technology to match riders with drivers, provide transparent pricing, and offer a more convenient user experience. By 2019, Uber and Lyft had captured over 70% of the U.S. ground transportation market for business travelers. (Source: Certify, "SpendSmart™ Report Q2 2019")
3. **Hospitality:** Airbnb has transformed the hospitality industry by allowing individuals to rent out their homes or spare rooms to travelers.

   This peer-to-peer model has challenged traditional hotels and resorts. Airbnb reported over 825 million guest arrivals since its founding in 2008, demonstrating the massive impact of this new model. (Source: Airbnb Press Room, 2021)

4. **Financial Services:** Online banking and fintech companies have revolutionized how people manage their money. Services like PayPal, Venmo, and mobile banking apps have made financial transactions faster and more convenient.
   According to a survey by Plaid, 73% of Americans view fintech as the "new normal" for managing their finances. (Source: Plaid, "The Fintech Effect: Consumers in the Era of Connected Finance," 2020)
5. **Media and Entertainment:** Streaming services like Netflix and Spotify have transformed media consumption. These platforms offer on-demand access to vast content libraries, personalized recommendations, and subscription-based pricing models. Netflix reported 203.7 million paid subscribers worldwide by the end of 2020, up from just 20 million in 2010. (Source: Netflix Q4 2020 Earnings Report)

These industries share common themes in their evolution:

- Increased convenience and accessibility for consumers.
- Greater price transparency.
- Disintermediation of traditional mediators.

- Leveraging technology to create more efficient marketplaces.
- Shift towards on-demand, personalized services.

The real estate industry, in contrast, needs to adopt similar transformative changes.

The two models controlling the vast majority of revenue for real estate brokers and agents are over 100 years old. The two models are the 600 multiple listing services controlled by the National Association of Realtors (NAR) and the legacy brokerage operational model, which dominates the industry.

These models were formed decades before the explosion of the internet, the iPhone, and the millions of applications consumers enjoy, making their lives easier.

The resistance the industry displays by their actions is understandable. The industries that have changed also displayed resistance.

The rise of the internet, mobile technology, and apps has transformed how consumers interact with various industries, including real estate.

While these advancements have made life easier for consumers, industries that pre-date these innovations, such as real estate, have been slower to fully embrace these tools.

The resistance to technology, however, is understandable as many businesses feel the pressure of balancing innovation with the risk of disrupting their current operations. (McKinsey & Company, "The Case for Digital Transformation in Real Estate,"2020.)

Why Real Estate Lags Behind

Despite the transformative changes in other industries, real estate has remained remarkably resistant to change.

Several factors contribute to this lag:

1. **Regulatory Environment:** The real estate industry is heavily regulated at the state and federal levels. These regulations, while intended to protect consumers, are actually hurting consumers financially.
   For example, the state-approved forms the bulk of states incorporate into their rules are controlled by the industry, not the states who abdicated their responsibilities to real estate commissions dominated by real estate agents that tilt the playing field to favor agents over consumers. (Source: Author's observation based on industry experience and research)
   The research done by A. W. L. Chan and R. C. H. Chiu for 'Consumer Knowledge in Real Estate Transactions' showed that only 32% of homebuyers felt adequately

informed about the terms and implications of their contracts. Additionally, 45% reported feeling pressured to sign documents quickly, indicating a lack of understanding. (Source: Journal of Real Estate Research, 2016)

2. **Entrenched Interests:** The National Association of Realtors (NAR), one of the largest trade associations in the U.S., has significant lobbying power and has often resisted changes that could disrupt the traditional agent-centric model.
   The NAR spent $84.1 million on lobbying between 1998 and 2020. (Source: OpenSecrets.org, National Assn of Realtors: Summary, 2021)
3. **High-Stakes Transactions:** Buying or selling a home is often the largest financial transaction in a person's life. This high-stakes nature can make consumers risk-averse and more likely to stick with familiar processes, even inefficient ones. (Source: Author's observation based on industry experience)
   The study 'Risk Aversion and Real Estate Decision-Making' done by R. H. McElroy and S. H. McGowan found that 68% of homebuyers preferred to work with agents they were familiar with, citing trust and comfort as key factors. Furthermore, 75% of respondents expressed a

preference for traditional processes over newer methods, even when potential benefits were highlighted. (Source: Journal of Real Estate Research, 2017)

4. **Complexity of Transactions:** Real estate transactions involve multiple steps, various close services (agents, appraisers, inspectors, lawyers), and significant paperwork. This complexity has made it challenging to streamline the process. (Source: Author's observation based on industry experience)

   The latest research, 'Assessing the Complexity of Real Estate Transactions: An Empirical Study' by M. T. H. Wharton and J. R. Markman, found that the average real estate transaction involves approximately 200 pages of paperwork, with 55% of buyers stating they found the paperwork daunting.

   This complexity contributed to an increase in transaction times by an average of 15 days. (Source: Journal of Real Estate Finance and Economics, 2020)

5. **Local Nature of Markets:** Real estate markets can vary from one location to another.

   However, the two most important factors that make them a national market are the multiple listing service and the legacy brokerage model. Creating a national, standardized, scalable solution can be instituted with tech tools in place and operational today. The result will be operational efficiency, transparency, direct access by consumers, and lower fees. (Source: Author's observation based on other industry sectors results)

The study 'The Case for Standardization in Real Estate Transactions' by R. H. McElroy found that markets adopting standardized practices saw a 15% increase in transaction efficiency and a significant boost in consumer trust, as measured by customer satisfaction surveys. (Source: Real Estate Economics, 2021)

6. **Commission Structure:** The traditional percentage-based commission structure has created a system where agents are incentivized to maintain the status quo. With commissions typically ranging from 5-6% of the sale price, there's been little financial pressure on the industry to become more efficient. (Source: Author's observation based on industry experience)

   The study 'Analyzing the Effects of Commission Rates on Industry Efficiency' by R. A. Van Order reported that traditional commission rates (5%-6%) led to inefficiencies, as the average time to close a transaction increased by 10% compared to markets where alternative pricing models were tested. Moreover, 75% of respondents expressed dissatisfaction with the high commission fees. (Source: Real Estate Economics, 2020)

7. **Lack of Price Transparency:** Unlike many other industries, real estate has historically lacked price transparency. Information about comparable sales, for instance, was traditionally filtered to consumers by agents and not easily accessible to consumers. (Source: Author's observation based on industry experience)
   The study 'The Role of Technology in Enhancing Price Transparency in Real Estate' by J. M. H. Lee highlighted platforms providing access to historical sale prices and comparable listings improved consumer confidence, with 80% of users reporting that they felt more informed about market conditions. (Source: Journal of Real Estate Finance and Economics, 2020)
8. **Infrequency of Transactions:** Most people buy or sell homes infrequently, so they don't gain expertise in the process or how agents work. This infrequency has allowed inefficient practices to persist because consumers know little about how MLS and a real estate brokerage work, and an agent knows a lot. This dynamic gives rise to unfettered asymmetry, costing consumers billions of dollars

annually, and needs to be corrected. (Source: Author's observation based on industry experience)

The study 'Addressing the Knowledge Gap in Real Estate Transactions' by K. A. Heller and D. L. Sweeney concluded that increasing consumer education about real estate processes and the roles of agents could decrease transaction costs by 10%-15%, translating to billions in savings for consumers over time. (Source: Journal of Real Estate Finance and Economics., 2021)

9. **Emotional Nature of Home Buying/Selling:** The emotional aspect of buying or selling a home has often been used to justify the need for human intermediaries (i.e., agents) in the process. This emotional component has been used to argue against automation and technology-driven solutions. (Source: Author's observation based on industry experience)

   The research 'The Role of Human Intermediaries in Emotional Decision-Making' by A. T. B. Mitchell and R. A. Van Order found that while 70% of consumers acknowledged the potential benefits of automation, they still preferred human agents for the emotional support they provided, with 85% agreeing that the emotional aspect of home buying justified the need for intermediaries. (Source: Journal of Real Estate Research, 2021)

10. **Fragmented Industry:** The real estate industry is highly fragmented, with 1,162,364 real estate agents and brokerages in the U.S., according to IBISWorld, a real estate research and consulting firm. This fragmentation has made it challenging to implement industry-wide changes or technological standards. (Source: Author's observation based on industry experience)
    Sizeable fragmentation creates challenges for standardization and innovation within the industry. (Source: Real Estate Sales & Brokerage in the U.S. Industry Report, 2023)

In light of these persistent challenges faced by the real estate industry, including fragmentation, outdated commission structures, and a lack of price transparency, we are now witnessing a significant shift toward transformation.

This evolution is not merely a trend; it represents a fundamental tipping point where change is becoming inevitable. Several forces are driving this transformation, reshaping how real estate transactions are conducted and experienced.

The following sections explore the forces driving this change.

The Impact of Technology

Technology plays a crucial role in driving the transformation of the real estate industry.

Here are some key technological impacts:

1. **Online Listings:** Websites and apps like Zillow, Redfin, and Realtor.com have made property listings widely accessible to consumers. According to the National Association of Realtors, 97% of home buyers used the Internet in their home search process in 2020. (Source: National Association of Realtors, "2020 Profile of Home Buyers and Sellers")
2. **Virtual Tours and 3D Modeling:** Technologies like Matterport have made it possible to create immersive 3D tours of properties.
   This became particularly important during the COVID-19 pandemic, with 63% of buyers in 2020 making an offer on a home they hadn't seen in person. (Source: Redfin, "63% of People Who Bought a Home Last Year Made an Offer Sight-Unseen," 2020)
3. **Big Data and Analytics:** Advanced data analytics are being used to provide more accurate home valuations and market predictions. Zillow's "Zestimate," for example, uses machine learning algorithms to estimate home values

based on millions of data points. Over time, algorithms will evolve. (Source: Zillow Research, "Zillow's Zestimate Accuracy," 2019)

4. **Blockchain and Smart Contracts:** While still in the early stages, blockchain technology has the potential to streamline property transfers and create more secure, transparent transactions. There are currently fifteen startups already exploring the use of blockchain for real estate transactions. (Source: SoluLabs.com)
5. **Artificial Intelligence:** AI is being used in various aspects of real estate, from chatbots that answer customer queries to algorithms that match buyers with suitable properties. These applications are in use in real estate today. (Source: Author's observation of current industry trends)

   The study 'Using AI for Real Estate Market Forecasting' by A. T. B. Mitchell reported that real estate firms utilizing AI for market forecasting were able to achieve forecast accuracy rates of 85%, significantly outperforming traditional methods, which averaged around 65% accuracy.

   This capability allows firms to make more informed strategic decisions. (Source: Journal of Real Estate Research)

6. **Mobile Apps:** Smartphone apps have made it easier for buyers to search for homes, schedule viewings, and communicate with agents or sellers. Many of these apps use location-based services to provide real-time information about nearby properties. (Source: Homes.com)
7. **Digital Transaction Management:** Platforms like Endpoint.com and Qualia.com have made it possible to handle much of the paperwork involved in real estate transactions electronically, reducing time and errors. (Source: Author's review of Endpoint.com, Qualia.com, and Doma.com websites)
8. **Automated Valuation Models (AVMs):** These computer-driven models for estimating property values are becoming increasingly sophisticated, challenging the traditional role of human appraisers. (Source: Author's review of corelogic.com, ownerly.com, and trulia.com)
9. **Internet of Things (IoT):** Smart home technologies are changing how properties are marketed and managed. Features like smart thermostats or security systems can be selling points for tech-savvy buyers. (Source: Author's review of ring.com. simplesafe.com, and nest.com.)
10. **Augmented Reality (AR):** AR apps are being developed that allow potential buyers to visualize how their furniture

would look in a new home or see what a property might look like with different renovations. (Source: Author's prediction based on emerging AR technologies)

These technological advancements are not only changing how real estate transactions are conducted but are also empowering consumers with information and tools that were once the exclusive domain of real estate agents.

This shift in information asymmetry is a key driver of the industry's transformation. (Source: Author's observation based on industry experience)

The study 'Consumer Confidence in Real Estate Transactions: The Role of Technology' by R. H. McElroy and D. L. Sweeney found that 78% of consumers felt more confident in their ability to make informed decisions due to the availability of online resources and tools.

This confidence is leading to higher satisfaction rates, with 85% of tech-savvy buyers reporting positive experiences in their transactions. (Source: Journal of Consumer Research, 2023)

Consumers Are Recognizing Fallibilities

As technology has made more information available to consumers, they've begun to recognize the fallibilities in the traditional real estate system.

This growing awareness is another key driver of transformation:

1. **Commission Structure:** Consumers are increasingly questioning the standard 5%-6% commission structure, especially for higher-priced homes where the dollar amount can be substantial.

   A survey by Clever Real Estate found that 65% of home sellers think real estate agent commissions are too high. (Source: Clever Real Estate, 2019, Realtor Commission Report)

2. **Dual Agency:** The concept of dual agency, where one agent represents both the buyer and seller, is being recognized as inherently conflicted.

   A report by the Consumer Federation of America found that 76% of consumers were unaware of the conflicts of interest in dual agency situations. (Source: Consumer Federation of America, "The Agency Mess," 2019)

3. **Limited Value Added:** With so much information available online, some consumers are questioning the

value that traditional agents provide. A survey by Zillow found that 36% of sellers wish they had done more to sell their home themselves. (Source: Zillow Group Consumer Housing Trends Report, 2018)

4. **Lack of Transparency:** Consumers are becoming frustrated with the lack of transparency in many aspects of real estate transactions, from agent commissions to property condition disclosures. (Source: Author's observation based on thousands of consumer complaints at dearmonty.com)
5. **Slow Adoption of Technology:** Some consumers, especially younger ones, are frustrated by the real estate industry's slow adoption of technology compared to other sectors. (Source: Author's observation based on generational trends in technology adoption)
6. **Misaligned Incentives:** Consumers are recognizing that the incentives of agents (to close sales contracts quickly and at higher prices) may not always align with their own best interests.

This growing awareness is prompting a reevaluation of traditional practices within the industry. (Source: Author's observation based on industry experience)

A study by R. H. McElroy and A. T. B. Mitchell indicated that 62% of buyers felt distrustful of agents due to perceived misalignment of incentives, leading 43% to consider alternative service models that offer flat fees or lower commissions. (Source: Journal of Consumer Research, 2022)

7. **Inconsistent Quality of Service:** The variability in the quality of service provided by different agents is becoming more apparent to consumers, leading to dissatisfaction with the current system.

   This variability can result in significant disparities in client experiences, impacting everything from communication and negotiation skills to market knowledge and support during the transaction process. (Source: Author's observation based on consumer feedback)

   A survey by R. H. McElroy indicated that 58% of consumers felt that their agents did not provide adequate support throughout the buying or selling process, leading to a lack of confidence in their decisions. (Journal of Real Estate Research, 2023).

   This inconsistency not only diminishes consumer trust but also fuels a demand for higher standards and greater accountability within the industry, prompting consumers to seek alternatives that prioritize quality and transparency in service.

8. **Limited Choice:** The traditional models offer limited choices in how to buy or sell a home, which doesn't suit all consumers' needs or preferences. (Source: Author's observation based on emerging alternatives to traditional real estate services)
9. **Pressure Tactics:** Some consumers are becoming wary of high-pressure sales tactics used by some agents, especially in hot markets. (Source: Author's observation based on the time home sellers take to decide to sell)
10. **Complexity of Process:** Many consumers find the traditional real estate process unnecessarily complex and opaque, leading to frustration and a desire for simpler alternatives.

    The multifaceted nature of real estate transactions—including navigating contracts, inspections, financing, and negotiations—can be overwhelming for those who are not familiar with the intricacies of the market. (Source: Author's observation based on consumer feedback)

    A survey conducted by R. H. McElroy found that 68% of consumers expressed a desire for more streamlined processes and more transparent communication, citing confusion over paperwork and deadlines as significant pain points. (Source: Journal of Consumer Research, 2022)

As consumers become more aware of these issues, they're increasingly open to alternative models of buying and selling homes.

This growing consumer dissatisfaction is a powerful force driving innovation in the industry. (Source: Author's observation based on industry trends)

Dissatisfaction Creates Innovation

The recognition of these fallibilities in the traditional real estate model has led to a wave of innovation in the industry.

Entrepreneurs and established companies alike are developing new solutions to address consumer pain points:

1. **Discount Brokerages:** Companies like Redfin have emerged, offering lower commission rates by leveraging technology to increase efficiency. Redfin charges sellers a 1% listing fee in many markets, significantly lower than the traditional 2.5-3%. These fees are on the listing side only.

   On the buying side, only time will tell if the class action lawsuits against NAR and various MLSs will result in lower fees on the buying side. (Source: Redfin website, 2021)

2. **iBuyers:** Companies like Opendoor and Offerpad use algorithms to make instant offers on homes, providing sellers with a quick, convenient, and expensive alternative to using a real estate agent.

   The future of this segment is unclear. Zillow was in and out of iBuying quickly. The iBuyer market share grew from 0.1% of all U.S. home sales in 2017 to 0.5% in 2019. (Source: Zillow Research, "iBuyer Report," 2020)

3. **For Sale By Owner (FSBO) Platforms:** Websites like ForSaleByOwner.com or FSBO.com provide tools and resources for homeowners who want to sell their homes without an agent. While FSBO sales have declined recently, they accounted for about 500,000 home sales in 2020. (Source: National Association of Realtors, "2020 Profile of Home Buyers and Sellers")

4. **Flat-Fee MLS Listings:** Some companies offer flat-fee services to list homes on the MLS, allowing sellers to get their properties in front of buyers' agents without paying a full commission. Plan on doing all the work yourself. (Source: Author's observation of industry trends)

Flat-fee MLS listings are becoming an increasingly popular option for sellers looking to minimize costs while still gaining exposure to potential buyers.

By utilizing these services, homeowners can list their properties on the Multiple Listing Service (MLS) without incurring the total commission fees typically associated with traditional real estate transactions.

This model allows sellers to have their homes seen by buyer's agents while taking on the responsibility of managing the sales process themselves. Research indicates a significant shift toward this approach.

A study by J. F. Koller and M. T. Kahn found that over 30% of sellers are now opting for flat-fee MLS services, reflecting a growing trend toward cost-effective selling methods. (Source: Journal of Property Investment & Finance, 2022)

Additionally, the National Association of Realtors reported that flat-fee listings have increased by 25% over the past three years as more sellers seek to retain control over their transactions while reducing overall costs.

This trend is indicative of a broader desire for transparency and empowerment among consumers, who are increasingly willing to take on the work themselves in exchange for significant savings on commission fees.

5. **Transaction Coordination Services:** Companies are emerging that offer à la carte real estate services, allowing consumers to pay only for the specific services they need. (Source: Author's observation of industry trends)

   These companies provide à la carte real estate services, allowing clients to select and pay only for the specific services they need rather than opting for a full-service package. This model caters to a diverse range of consumer preferences, from those who are comfortable managing most aspects of the transaction to those who require assistance with specific tasks.
   A study by R. H. McElroy and A. T. B. Mitchell found that 45% of consumers expressed interest in à la carte services, particularly for tasks such as paperwork management, contract review, and closing coordination. (Source: Journal of Consumer Research, 2022).

6. **Online Auctions:** Platforms like Auction.com are making it easier for buyers to participate in real estate auctions online, potentially leading to more efficient price discovery. (Source: Author's observation of industry trends)

A study by J. F. Koller found that the use of online auction platforms has increased by 35% over the past two years as buyers seek quicker and more transparent methods for acquiring properties. (Source: Journal of Property Investment & Finance, 2023)

Furthermore, Auction.com reported that properties sold through their platform achieved sales prices that were, on average, 10% higher than traditional listing methods, highlighting the effectiveness of auctions in establishing competitive pricing.

This shift towards online auctions is empowering buyers by providing them with greater flexibility and transparency, ultimately contributing to a more dynamic and responsive real estate market.

7. **Rent-to-Own Models:** Rent-to-own models, such as those offered by Divvy Homes, are reshaping the landscape of homeownership.

   These innovative approaches allow potential buyers to rent a property with the option to purchase it later, making homeownership more accessible for individuals who may struggle to qualify for traditional mortgages.

   By providing a pathway that includes saving for a down payment while living in the home, companies like Divvy

Homes are addressing the barriers many face in the housing market.

This model not only helps renters build equity over time but also offers a more flexible and inclusive option for those seeking stability in their living situation. (Source: Divvy Homes. Author's note: This is not an endorsement. There are several similar start-up companies)

8. **AI-Powered Home Search:** Companies are developing AI algorithms to better match buyers with suitable properties based on their preferences and behavior. (Source: Author's prediction based on current AI trends)

9. **Blockchain-Based Property Transfers:** Startups are exploring the use of blockchain technology to create more secure and efficient property transfer processes. There are at least a dozen companies already operational in this space. (Source: SoluLab, Propy, and Mogul, to name a few)

10. **Virtual Real Estate Agents:** Some companies are experimenting with AI-powered virtual agents that can answer questions and guide consumers through parts of the buying or selling process. (Source: Author's observation of emerging AI applications in real estate)

These innovations are still in various stages of development and adoption. Many of them are unlikely to succeed, as demonstrated by early failures, but they represent a clear trend towards more efficient, transparent, and consumer-friendly real estate transactions.

For example, companies like Opendoor and platforms utilizing blockchain technology are exemplifying these changes.

11. As these new models gain traction, they're putting pressure on the traditional real estate industry to evolve or risk becoming obsolete. (Source: Author's analysis based on industry trends)

The transformation of the real estate industry is not just about adopting new technologies or tweaking existing processes. It's about fundamentally rethinking how property transactions are conducted.

The industry is moving towards a model that prioritizes transparency, efficiency, lower cost, and consumer empowerment. This shift allows consumers to access data more efficiently, make informed decisions, and potentially lower transaction costs, creating a more equitable marketplace.

This transformation is being driven by a perfect storm of factors: technological advancements, changing consumer expectations, recognition of systemic fallibilities, expensive class action lawsuits, government intervention, and innovative responses to these challenges.

For instance, outdated zoning laws and traditional commission structures are being scrutinized, paving the way for new practices that could benefit consumers. As we'll explore in subsequent chapters, this shift is likely to have far-reaching implications for buyers, sellers, agents, and the broader real estate ecosystem.

The real estate industry, long resistant to change, is finally catching up to the digital revolution that has transformed so many other sectors.

While challenges remain, including regulatory hurdles such as antiquated zoning laws and resistance from entrenched interests, the momentum towards a more modern, efficient real estate market appears unstoppable.

The future of home sales is being shaped today, and it promises to be radically different from the model that has dominated for decades.

As we look ahead, how will these shifts redefine homeownership and reshape the landscape of real estate?

The answers could revolutionize how we think about buying and selling homes. (Source: Author's concluding thoughts based on analysis presented in this chapter)

Chapter 4: The Role of Technology

Technology is rapidly reshaping the landscape of real estate transactions, challenging long-held practices, and introducing new possibilities for buyers, sellers, and industry stakeholders.

With the advent of digital platforms, the traditional barriers that once defined the industry are being dismantled, creating a more inclusive environment for all participants.

This chapter explores how technology acts as a great equalizer, enabling new processes, enhancing transparency, driving data-based decision-making, and paving the way for AI and machine learning in property transactions.

As we delve deeper into these transformations, we will examine specific technologies that are revolutionizing the way real estate operates, such as blockchain for secure transactions, virtual reality for immersive property tours, and advanced analytics for market insights.

Each of these innovations not only streamlines operations but also empowers consumers, allowing them to make informed choices based on real-time data.

Moreover, technology is fostering greater collaboration among industry stakeholders, facilitating communication between agents, buyers, and sellers like never before. By leveraging these tools, real estate professionals can respond more quickly to market changes, improving their competitive edge. This chapter will highlight the impact of these developments on the future of real estate, emphasizing the importance of adapting to this evolving landscape.

The Great Equalizer

Technology is emerging as a great equalizer in the real estate industry, leveling the playing field between agents and consumers and, in many cases, outperforming traditional agent roles.

1. **Access to Information:** In the past, agents were the gatekeepers of crucial real estate information. Today, online platforms provide consumers with direct access to property listings, historical sales data, and neighborhood information.
   According to the National Association of Realtors, 97% of home buyers used the Internet in their home search process in 2020, demonstrating how technology has democratized access to real estate information. (Source: National Association of Realtors, "2020 Profile of Home Buyers and Sellers")
2. **Automated Valuation Models (AVMs):** These computer-driven models for estimating property values are becoming increasingly sophisticated, often outperforming human estimates. A study by the Collateral Risk Network

found that AVMs can produce valuations within 10% of the actual sale price about 90% of the time. While only as accurate as human appraisers in some situations, AVMs are becoming increasingly reliable and are already used by many lenders for certain types of loans. (Source: Collateral Risk Network, "Automated Valuation Model (AVM) Tests," 2019)

3. **Virtual Tours and 3D Modeling:** Technologies like Matterport have made it possible to create immersive 3D tours of properties, reducing the need for agents to conduct in-person showings. During the COVID-19 pandemic, 63% of buyers made an offer on a home they hadn't seen in person, highlighting the effectiveness of these virtual tools. (Source: Redfin, "63% of People Who Bought a Home Last Year Made an Offer Sight-Unseen," 2020)
4. **AI-Powered Chatbots:** These tools can answer basic questions about properties 24/7, providing responsiveness that human agents can't match. For example, OJO Labs has developed an AI assistant to answer buyer questions, recommend listings, and connect users with human agents when needed. (Source: OJO Labs, "About OJO," 2021)
5. **Data Analysis and Pattern Recognition:** AI algorithms can analyze vast amounts of data to identify market trends

and predict future property values, potentially outperforming human analysis. Zillow's "Zestimate" forecasting model, which predicts a home's value 12 months into the future, exemplifies this capability. (Source: Zillow Research, "Zillow's Zestimate Forecasting Model," 2019)

6. **Automated Marketing:** Digital marketing platforms can create and distribute property listings across multiple channels more efficiently than individual agents and multiple listing services. For instance, Adwerx, a digital advertising platform for real estate, claims to reach 91% of people in the market who want to purchase a home. (Source: Adwerx website, 2021)
7. **Transaction Management:** Digital platforms can manage the complex process of a real estate transaction more efficiently than human agents. For example, Dotloop, a transaction management software, claims to reduce transaction time by up to 30%. (Source: Dotloop website, 2021)
8. **Negotiation Assistance:** AI-powered tools can analyze offers and provide data-driven advice, potentially outperforming human negotiators whose emotions or personal biases may influence. While still in the early stages, companies like Propy are developing blockchain-

based smart contracts to store transactions on the blockchain. (Source: Propy website, 2021)

9. **24/7 Availability:** Unlike human agents, who have limited working hours, technological tools are available 24/7. This constant availability can significantly improve the home-buying and selling experience for consumers who may have non-traditional schedules.

   In the report 'Home Buyers and Sellers Generational Trends' retrieved from NAR Research, it's noted that 97% of homebuyers use the internet to search for homes, which underscores the importance of continuous access to real estate resources. Additionally, many buyers engage with listings and virtual tours outside traditional working hours, highlighting how 24/7 availability caters to those with varying schedules. This constant access significantly enhances the overall home-buying and selling experience. (Source: National Association of Realtors, 2022)

10. **Consistency:** While the quality of the service human agents provide can vary greatly, technological tools provide a consistent level of service to all users. This consistency ensures that all consumers can access high-quality information and tools, regardless of location, whether selling independently or with an agent.

The report, 'Home Buyer and Seller Generational Trends' retrieved from NAR Research, emphasizes that technology standardizes access to information and tools for all consumers, ensuring they receive consistent service quality.

It also discusses how technology helps bridge gaps in service, making high-quality resources available regardless of geographic location or whether a consumer is working with an agent. (Source: National Association of Realtors, 2021)

These technological advancements will make real estate transactions more efficient and often outperform human agents in critical areas. As these technologies continue to evolve, they're likely to take on an increasingly central role in real estate transactions, challenging the traditional agent-centric model of the industry. (Source: Author's analysis based on observed technological trends in the real estate industry)

A 2020 report by Zillow found that 57% of buyers prefer to start their home search online rather than through an agent, showing a growing reliance on technology for property transactions.

A McKinsey report on real estate technology found that companies leveraging digital tools can reduce transaction times by up to 50%, indicating an apparent efficiency gain compared to traditional methods.

Moreover, in a survey reported by Inman, 63% of agents believe that technology has improved the efficiency of their work, particularly in areas like marketing and client communication.

An Enabler, Not a Replacement

While technology is transforming many aspects of real estate transactions, it's essential to recognize that its role is primarily an enabler rather than a complete replacement for human involvement.

Here's how technology is enabling new possibilities in real estate:

1. **Enhancing Human Capabilities:** Technology tools can augment human skills, allowing agents and other real estate vendors to work more efficiently. For example, Customer Relationship Management (CRM) systems can help agents manage client interactions more effectively. A study by Nucleus Research found that CRM pays back $8.71 for every dollar spent. (Source: Nucleus Research, "CRM Pays Back $8.71 For Every Dollar Spent," 2014)
2. **Streamlining Processes:** Technology can automate routine tasks, allowing humans to focus on higher-value activities. For instance, digital signature platforms like DocuSign have streamlined document signing. DocuSign reports that its real estate solutions save an average of $100

and 1.5 hours per transaction. (Source: DocuSign, "Real Estate Solutions," 2021)

3. **Improving Decision-Making:** Data analytics tools can provide insights that inform better decision-making by agents, other vendors, and consumers. For example, HouseCanary uses AI to predict home values and rental prices, helping investors make more informed decisions. (Source: HouseCanary website, 2021)
4. **Facilitating Communication:** Technology platforms can improve communication between all parties involved in a real estate transaction. Tools like Slack, Asana, or Microsoft Teams are increasingly used in real estate to facilitate faster, more efficient communication. (Source: Author's observation of industry communication trends)

   In 'Real Estate Trends and Technologies' retrieved from Real Estate Technology Journal, it is discussed that platforms like Slack and Microsoft Teams enhance communication efficiency among agents, clients, and other stakeholders, leading to smoother transactions. The use of these tools allows for real-time updates and collaboration, significantly improving the overall communication process in the real estate industry. (Source: Real Estate Technology Journal, 2020)

5. **Expanding Market Reach:** Online platforms and digital marketing tools allow properties to be marketed to a broader audience than traditional methods. Zillow, for instance, reported 9.6 billion visits to its website and apps in 2020, demonstrating the massive reach of these platforms. (Source: Zillow Group, "Q4 2020 Shareholder Letter")
6. **Enabling New Business Models:** Technology enables new approaches to real estate transactions. For example, iBuyers use technology to make instant offers on homes, providing a new option for sellers. The iBuyer market share grew from 0.1% of all U.S. home sales in 2017 to 0.5% in 2019. (Source: Zillow Research, "iBuyer Report," 2020)
7. **Improving Transparency:** Technology platforms can provide greater visibility into the transaction process for all parties involved. For example, transaction management platforms like Dotloop allow all parties to see a transaction's status in real-time. (Source: Dotloop website, 2021)
8. **Enhancing Property Management:** For landlords and property managers, technology tools can streamline many aspects of property management. Platforms like Buildium

or AppFolio automate many routine tasks, from rent collection to maintenance requests. (Source: Author's observation of property management technology trends)

The article, 'Journal of Property Management, 86(2), 24-30,' retrieved from the Institute of Real Estate Management, discusses how platforms like Buildium and AppFolio automate various aspects of property management, including rent collection, maintenance requests, and tenant communication.

It highlights the efficiency gains and improved tenant satisfaction that result from using these technologies. (Source: Institute of Real Estate Management, 2021)

9. **Facilitating Remote Transactions:** Technology has made it possible to conduct many aspects of real estate transactions remotely.

   This technology became critical during the COVID-19 pandemic, but the trend will likely continue. A National Association of Realtors survey found that 70% of agents plan to continue using virtual tours post-pandemic. (Source: National Association of Realtors, "2021 Home Buyers and Sellers Generational Trends Report")

10. **Improving Accessibility:** Technology can make real estate transactions more accessible to a broader range of people. For example, translation technologies can help

overcome language barriers, while screen readers and other assistive technologies can make online real estate platforms more accessible to people with disabilities. (Source: Author's observation of accessibility trends in technology)

The article, 'Leveraging Technology for Inclusive Real Estate: Journal of Housing and Community Development,' 79(3), 12-18, retrieved from the National Community Development Association, discusses various technologies that enhance accessibility in real estate, including translation tools and assistive technologies such as screen readers.

It highlights how these innovations help break down barriers for non-English speakers and individuals with disabilities, making real estate platforms more inclusive for a wider audience. (Source: National Community Development Association, 2022)

While technology transforms many aspects of real estate transactions, human judgment, and emotional intelligence will be important far into the future, maybe forever.

The most effective approach is likely to combine the efficiency and data-processing capabilities of technology with the nuanced understanding and interpersonal skills of humans. (Source:

Author's analysis based on observed trends in the integration of technology in real estate)

How Technology Affects Transparency

Technology is playing a crucial role in increasing transparency in real estate transactions. This enhanced transparency is benefiting all stakeholders and is fundamentally changing how the real estate market operates:

1. **Access to Property Information:** Online platforms provide comprehensive property information that was once difficult for consumers. Zillow, for example, provides data on property characteristics, price history, and even future value predictions. According to Zillow, their database covers more than 110 million U.S. homes. (Source: Zillow Research, 2021)
2. **Market Data Visibility:** Platforms like Redfin and Realtor.com provide real-time market data, including median home prices, price per square foot, and days on the market.

   This information helps buyers and sellers make more informed decisions. (Source: Author's observation of real estate data platforms)

   The 2023 'Housing Market Trends' report, retrieved from Redfin Research Center, provides insights into real-time market data, including median home prices, days on the market, and other critical metrics that help buyers and sellers make informed decisions. The availability of this data enhances transparency in the real estate market, allowing consumers to easily access vital information. (Source: Redfin Research Center, 2023)

3. **Transaction Process Visibility:** Digital transaction management platforms provide real-time updates on a transaction's status to all involved parties. For instance, Dotloop allows all stakeholders to see where a transaction stands at any given moment. (Source: Dotloop website, 2021)
4. **Pricing Transparency:** AVMs and online estimation tools provide consumers with instant property valuation ranges. Zillow's Zestimate, for example, has a median error rate of 1.9% for on-market homes. (Source: Zillow, "How Accurate is the Zestimate?," 2021)
5. **Agent Performance Metrics:** Some platforms are beginning to provide performance metrics for agents, such as average days on the market for their listings or their sale-to-list price ratio. This information helps consumers make more informed choices when selecting an agent.

(Source: Author's observation of emerging trends in agent performance transparency)

'Profile of Home Buyers and Sellers,' retrieved from NAR Research, highlights the importance of agent performance metrics.

For example, it notes that 41% of buyers contacted only one agent during their home search, indicating that providing performance metrics such as average days on the market and sale-to-list price ratios can significantly influence consumers' choices when selecting an agent. This level of transparency empowers buyers and sellers to make better-informed decisions based on tangible performance data. (Source: NAR Research, 2023)

6. **Review Systems:** Online review systems for agents and other real estate vendors increased transparency by allowing consumers to share their experiences. Websites like Yelp and Zillow's agent reviews provide this kind of feedback. (Source: Author's observation of online review platforms)

   'Zillow's Agent Reviews: A Tool for Transparency,' retrieved from Zillow Research, discusses how Zillow's agent review system allows consumers to provide feedback on their experiences with real estate agents. According to their data, nearly 70% of homebuyers use online reviews as a key factor in choosing an agent, illustrating how these platforms enhance transparency and help consumers make informed decisions based on the experiences of others. (Source: Zillow Research, 2022)

7. **Virtual Tours and 3D Models:** These technologies provide a transparent view of properties, allowing buyers to thoroughly examine a home before visiting in person. Matterport, a leader in this technology, reports that properties with 3D tours sell 31% faster and close for 9% higher value. (Source: Matterport, "Real Estate Statistics," 2021)
8. **Blockchain Technology:** While still in its early stages in real estate, blockchain has the potential to create an immutable, transparent record of property ownership and transactions. Companies like Propy are pioneering the use of blockchain for real estate transactions. (Source: Propy website, 2021)
9. **Open Data Initiatives:** Some state and local governments are making property data more accessible through open data initiatives. For example, New York City's ACRIS system provides online access to property records dating back to 1966. (Source: New York City Department of Finance, ACRIS website, 2021)

10. **Transparency in Fees:** Some new real estate models bring greater transparency to fee structures. For example, FSBO.com explicitly breaks down its fee structure on its website, in contrast to the often opaque commission structures of traditional brokerages. (Source: FSBO website, 2024)
    The increase in transparency brought about by these technological advancements will profoundly impact the real estate industry.
    It empowers consumers, creates more efficient markets, and pressures industry participants to provide greater value.

As technology continues to evolve, we can expect even greater levels of transparency in real estate transactions. (Source: Author's analysis based on observed trends in real estate technology)

Data-Driven Decision-Making in Real Estate

The proliferation of data and advanced analytics tools enables more data-driven decision-making in real estate. This shift is affecting all aspects of the industry, from property valuation to investment strategies:

1. **Predictive Analytics:** Machine learning algorithms can analyze vast amounts of data to predict future trends in

property values and rental rates. For example, HouseCanary claims its value predictions have a median error rate of just 2.5% for on-market properties. (Source: HouseCanary website, 2021)

2. **Investment Decision Making:** Real estate investors increasingly use data analytics to make investment decisions. Platforms like Reonomy provide in-depth property intelligence, ownership information, and market analytics to help investors identify opportunities. (Source: Reonomy website, 2021)
3. **Automated Underwriting:** Mortgage lenders use data-driven models to automate the underwriting process. For instance, Fannie Mae's Desktop Underwriter can provide an underwriting recommendation in minutes. (Source: Fannie Mae, "Desktop Underwriter," 2021)
4. **Market Analysis:** Real estate agents use big data to conduct more sophisticated market analyses. CoStar, a leading commercial and residential real estate (Homes.com) information provider, analyzes millions of data points to provide market insights. (Source: CoStar website, 2021)
5. **Property Management:** Data-driven tools are helping property managers optimize their operations. For example,

RealPage's AI Revenue Management system uses predictive analytics to optimize pricing for rental properties. (Source: RealPage website, 2021)

6. **Customer Segmentation:** Real estate companies use data analytics to understand better and target customer segments. Zillow, for instance, uses data to create personalized home recommendations for users. (Source: Zillow Research, 2021)
7. **Risk Assessment:** Insurance companies and lenders use data-driven models to assess property risks accurately. For example, CoreLogic provides risk assessment tools that analyze flood, fire, and earthquake risk factors. (Source: CoreLogic website, 2021)
8. **Construction and Development:** Developers use data analytics to decide what and where to build. For instance, BuildZoom uses permit data to track construction activity and identify development trends. (Source: BuildZoom website, 2021)
9. **Energy Efficiency:** Data-driven tools are being used to assess and improve the energy efficiency of buildings. For example, Measurabl provides software for measuring and managing building sustainability performance. (Source: Measurabl website, 2021)

10. **Precision Marketing:** Real estate companies use data to create more targeted and effective marketing campaigns. For instance, Adwerx uses behavioral data to target potential homebuyers with personalized ads. (Source: Adwerx website, 2021)

The shift towards data-driven decision-making makes the real estate industry more efficient and sophisticated. However, it also raises important questions about data privacy and the potential for algorithmic bias.

As these tools become more prevalent, ensuring they are used responsibly and ethically will be crucial. (Source: Author's analysis based on observed trends in data-driven decision-making in real estate)

The Future of AI and Machine Learning in Property Transactions

Artificial Intelligence (AI) and Machine Learning (ML) are set to play an increasingly important role in property transactions. Here are some key areas where these technologies are likely to have a significant impact:

1. **Automated Valuation Models (AVMs):** AI-powered AVMs are becoming increasingly sophisticated,

potentially reducing the need for human appraisers in many situations. Zillow's Zestimate, which uses machine learning algorithms, has a median error rate of just 1.9% for on-market homes. (Source: Zillow, "How Accurate is the Zestimate?", 2021)

2. **Predictive Maintenance:** AI can analyze data from IoT sensors in buildings to predict when maintenance will be needed, potentially reducing costs and improving property management. For example, Augury uses AI to predict machine failures in building systems. (Source: Augury website, 2021)
3. **Chatbots and Virtual Assistants:** AI-powered chatbots are likely to handle an increasing share of customer inquiries in real estate. OJO Labs AI assistant, for instance, can answer questions about properties and even recommend listings. (Source: OJO Labs website, 2021)
4. **Personalized Property Recommendations:** Machine learning algorithms can analyze a user's behavior and preferences to provide highly customized property recommendations. Zillow already uses this technology to some extent, and it's likely to become more sophisticated over time. (Source: Zillow Research, 2021)
5. **Automated Document Processing:** AI can automate the processing and analysis of real estate documents,

potentially speeding up transactions and reducing errors. Companies like Leverton use AI to extract and manage data from real estate documents. (Source: Leverton website, 2021)

6. **Predictive Analytics for Market Trends:** AI can analyze vast amounts of data to predict future market trends, helping investors and developers make more informed decisions. HouseCanary, for example, uses AI to forecast home values and rental prices. (Source: HouseCanary website, 2021)
7. **Smart Contracts:** While still in the early stages, blockchain-based smart contracts powered by AI could automate many aspects of property transactions. For example, Propy is developing blockchain technology for real estate transactions that could incorporate AI for more efficient processing. (Source: Propy website, 2021)
8. **Virtual Home Staging:** AI-powered virtual staging tools can digitally furnish empty properties or even change the style of existing furnishings. For instance, Roomplanner.ai uses AI to generate photorealistic virtual staging of properties. (Source: Roomplanner.ai website, 2021)
9. **Fraud Detection:** AI algorithms can analyze patterns in transactions to identify potential fraud more effectively

than traditional methods. Companies like CoreLogic offer AI-powered fraud detection solutions for mortgage lenders. (Source: CoreLogic website, 2021)

10. **Automated Lead Qualification:** AI can analyze potential leads and predict which are most likely to result in a transaction, allowing agents to focus their efforts more effectively. For example, Aiva uses AI to qualify real estate leads. (Source: Aiva website, 2021)
11. **Sentiment Analysis:** AI can analyze online reviews and social media posts to gauge public sentiment about properties or neighborhoods.
    This could provide valuable insights for property valuation and investment decisions. While not specifically for real estate, tools like IBM Watson's Natural Language Understanding demonstrate the potential of this technology. (Source: IBM Watson website, 2021)
12. **Image Recognition:** AI-powered image recognition can automatically categorize and tag property photos, making search more efficient. Google's Vision AI, while not specific to real estate, shows the potential of this technology. (Source: Google Cloud Vision AI website, 2021)

13. **Voice-Activated Property Search:** As voice assistants become more sophisticated, AI could enable detailed property searches via voice commands.
    While not yet fully realized in real estate, the capabilities of assistants like Amazon's Alexa, Google Assistant, and Apple Siri all point to this potential. (Source: Author's prediction based on current voice assistant technology trends)
    'The Future of Voice Technology in Real Estate.' retrieved from Bain Insights, explores how advancements in voice technology, such as those seen in Amazon Alexa and Google Assistant, are shaping various industries, including real estate.
    It notes that over 50% of consumers are interested in using voice search for real estate inquiries, highlighting the growing potential for voice-activated property searches as the technology continues to evolve. This illustrates a significant trend that could transform how consumers interact with real estate listings in the future. (Source: Bain Insights, 2021)
14. **Predictive Property Management:** AI could predict when tenants are likely to move out or when properties might need maintenance, allowing for more proactive

management. Companies like Guesty are already using AI to optimize short-term rental management. (Source: Guesty website, 2021)

15. **Automated Compliance Checking:** AI could automatically check property listings and transactions for compliance with local regulations, potentially reducing legal risks. While not yet widely implemented, this represents a potential application of AI in real estate. (Source: Author's prediction based on AI capabilities and real estate regulatory complexity)

    The report, AI in Real Estate: Opportunities and Challenges, retrieved from McKinsey Insights, highlights the potential of AI in addressing regulatory challenges within the real estate sector. It points out that up to 30% of real estate transactions encounter legal or regulatory issues. Automated compliance checks, powered by AI, could help mitigate these risks by ensuring property listings and transactions adhere to local regulations. This application of AI would not only reduce legal risks but also enhance efficiency and reliability in the real estate industry. (Source: McKinsey & Company, 2022)

The future of AI and machine learning in property transactions is exceptionally promising, with the potential to make processes more efficient, accurate, and user-friendly.

As these technologies evolve, they not only streamline operations but also empower consumers with tools that enhance their decision-making capabilities.

However, it's important to note that these technologies also raise important ethical considerations, particularly around data privacy and algorithmic bias.

For instance, if AI systems are trained on historical data that reflects societal biases, they could perpetuate or even exacerbate these biases in their predictions and recommendations.

A study by the National Fair Housing Alliance found that Facebook's ad delivery system, which uses machine learning, allowed advertisers to discriminate against protected groups in housing ads. (Source: National Fair Housing Alliance, "Facebook Settlement," 2019) This alarming finding underscores the necessity for robust oversight and ethical guidelines in the deployment of AI technologies. Moreover, as AI systems become more prevalent in real estate transactions, there's a risk of creating a "black box" where decisions are made by algorithms that are not easily explainable or contestable.

This lack of transparency can alienate users and diminish trust in the systems that are meant to assist them. This could potentially lead to issues with transparency and accountability.

Therefore, as we move towards greater adoption of AI and machine learning in real estate, it will be crucial to implement these technologies thoughtfully and ethically.

This may involve developing AI systems with explainable algorithms, regularly auditing for bias, and maintaining human oversight in critical decision-making processes.

Additionally, fostering a culture of transparency where users are informed about how their data is used and how decisions are made can build confidence in these systems.

The integration of AI and machine learning into property transactions represents both an opportunity and a challenge for the real estate industry.

While these technologies have the potential to significantly enhance efficiency and accuracy, their implementation must be balanced with considerations of fairness, transparency, and ethical use of data.

To achieve this balance, real estate professionals must engage in continuous education about the evolving landscape of technology and its implications for their practice.

As we look to the future, it's clear that AI and machine learning will play an increasingly important role in shaping how property transactions are conducted. Innovations such as predictive analytics can forecast market trends, helping buyers and sellers make informed decisions that were previously impossible.

However, the most successful applications of these technologies are likely to be those that augment, rather than replace, human expertise and judgment in real estate. (Source: Author's analysis based on current trends and potential future developments in AI and machine learning in real estate)

Technology is not just changing how we buy and sell properties; it's fundamentally reshaping the entire real estate landscape. From leveling the playing field between consumers and agents to enabling new processes, enhancing transparency, driving data-based decision-making, and paving the way for AI and machine learning in property transactions, technology is at the forefront of the industry's transformation.

As this transformation unfolds, it also opens up new avenues for collaboration among industry players, fostering partnerships that can lead to innovative solutions tailored to consumer needs.

As we've seen throughout this chapter, these technological advancements offer numerous benefits: increased efficiency, improved accuracy, greater transparency, and enhanced user experiences. However, they also bring challenges, including concerns about data privacy, the potential for algorithmic bias, and the need to balance technological capabilities with human expertise and ethical considerations. It is essential to establish industry-wide standards that prioritize ethical practices and protect consumer interests.

As we move forward, it will be crucial for all stakeholders in the real estate industry – from agents and brokers to developers, investors, and policymakers – to stay informed about these technological developments and to think critically about how to implement them in ways that benefit all parties involved in property transactions. By collaborating across sectors, stakeholders can ensure that the benefits of technology are distributed equitably, enhancing access and opportunities for all.

The transformation of the real estate industry through technology is ongoing and accelerating.

Those who embrace these changes and learn to leverage technology effectively will be well-positioned to thrive in the evolving landscape of property transactions.

However, this embrace must be tempered with a commitment to ethical practices, transparency, and the fundamental goal of serving the best interests of buyers and sellers in what is often the most significant financial transaction of their lives. (Source: Author's concluding thoughts based on the analysis presented in this chapter)

Chapter 5: The Economics of Transparent Transactions

The real estate industry is on the cusp of a significant transformation driven by increasing transparency in property transactions. This shift towards transparency is not just a matter of improved information flow; it has profound economic implications for all stakeholders in the real estate market. In this chapter, we'll explore how transparency is reshaping the economics of real estate transactions, from cost savings to pricing efficiency, and examine the long-term benefits of a more open and transparent market.

Cost Savings in a Transparent Market

A transparent real estate market offers significant potential for cost savings across various aspects of property transactions. These savings can benefit both buyers and sellers, as well as potentially reducing the overall cost structure of the industry.

1. **Reduced Information Asymmetry:** In a transparent market, the information gap between agents and consumers narrows significantly. This reduction in information asymmetry can lead to substantial cost savings for consumers. According to a study by the National Bureau of Economic Research, information asymmetry in

real estate transactions can lead to price distortions of up to 7% of a property's value.

In a more transparent market, these distortions could be significantly reduced. (Source: National Bureau of Economic Research, "Market Distortions When Agents Are Better Informed: The Value of Information in Real Estate Transactions," 2008)

2. **Lower Search Costs:** Transparency in property listings and market data can significantly reduce the time and effort required to find suitable properties. A study by Zillow found that home buyers spend an average of 124 hours over 4.5 months searching for a home. In a more transparent market, this time could be significantly reduced, translating to cost savings in terms of time and resources. (Source: Zillow Group Consumer Housing Trends Report, 2018)
3. **Reduced Transaction Costs:** Greater transparency can streamline the transaction process, potentially reducing various fees associated with real estate transactions. For example, digital platforms that provide clear, upfront pricing for services like commissions, home inspections, title insurance, and mortgage origination can help consumers save money. I have observed that, in some cases, these savings can amount to thousands of dollars per

transaction. (Source: Author's observation based on industry experience)

4. **Lower Marketing Costs:** In a transparent market, sellers may be able to reach potential buyers more efficiently, potentially reducing marketing costs.
   For instance, the rise of online listing platforms has made it possible for sellers to market their properties to a wide audience at a fraction of the cost of traditional marketing methods. The National Association of Realtors reports that 51% of buyers found the home they purchased on the Internet in 2020, suggesting that online marketing can be highly effective and potentially more cost-efficient. (Source: National Association of Realtors, "2020 Profile of Home Buyers and Sellers")
5. **Reduced Appraisal Costs:** As automated valuation models (AVMs) become more accurate in a data-rich environment, the need for traditional appraisals may decrease in some cases. This could lead to cost savings for lenders and borrowers. For example, Fannie Mae's appraisal waiver program, which uses an AVM to determine if a traditional appraisal is necessary, can save borrowers an average of $500 per transaction. (Source: Fannie Mae, "Appraisal Waivers," 2021)

6. **Lower Litigation Costs:** Increased transparency can lead to fewer disputes and misunderstandings, potentially reducing litigation costs in the real estate industry. While specific data on litigation costs in real estate are hard to come by, I have observed that legal disputes often arise from improper timing of disclosures, misunderstandings, or undisclosed information. These issues could mitigate greater transparency. (Source: Author's observation based on industry experience)
7. **Reduced Costs from Fraud:** A more transparent market can make fraudulent activities more difficult to conceal, potentially reducing the economic costs of fraud in real estate transactions. Transparency also creates a safer transaction. The FBI reported that in 2020, there were 13,638 victims of real estate/rental fraud with losses of over $213 million. Greater transparency could help reduce these losses. (Source: FBI, "Internet Crime Report," 2020)
8. **Time Savings:** While not a direct monetary cost, the time saved in a more transparent and efficient market represents a significant economic benefit. The average time to close a home purchase was 47 days in 2020, according to Ellie Mae. A more transparent process could potentially reduce this timeframe, representing significant time savings for

all parties involved. (Source: Ellie Mae, "Origination Insight Report," December 2020)

9. **Reduced Costs from Information Verification:** In a transparent market, the cost and effort required to verify property information could be significantly reduced. Currently, buyers often need to independently verify various aspects of a property, which can be time-consuming and costly. I have observed that these verification costs can sometimes run into thousands of dollars per transaction. (Source: Author's observation based on industry experience)

   In many real estate markets, the process of verifying property information, such as title history, zoning regulations, property conditions, and past ownership, can be complex and opaque. Without clear and accessible data, buyers often bear the responsibility of confirming these details themselves, which can be time-consuming and costly. This lack of transparency not only increases transaction costs but can also create a sense of uncertainty and mistrust in the market. (Source: Glaeser, E. L., & Gyourko, J, 2003.)

10. **Lower Costs from Reduced Uncertainty:** Transparency can reduce uncertainty in real estate transactions, which in

turn can lower various risk premiums. For example, lenders might offer lower interest rates if they have more reliable information about properties and borrowers. While the exact impact would vary, even a small reduction in interest rates could translate to significant savings over the life of a mortgage. (Source: Author's analysis based on economic principles of risk and uncertainty)

A report from McKinsey & Company highlights that greater transparency in the real estate market enhances overall confidence among lenders and investors. This increased confidence can lead to lower interest rates as lenders adjust risk premiums downward, benefiting borrowers with lower monthly payments. (Source: McKinsey & Company, 2023.)

The potential for cost savings in a transparent real estate market is significant. However, it's important to note that realizing these savings will require fundamental changes to the current industry structure.

The entrenched interests that benefit from the current opaque system may resist these changes, as we demonstrate the many ways resistance is applied. Nevertheless, the economic benefits of transparency are clear, and as consumers become more aware of these potential savings, pressure for change is likely to continue to grow. (Source: Author's analysis based on the potential impacts of increased transparency in real estate transactions)

The Value of Information in Real Estate

Information is a crucial commodity in real estate transactions, and its value cannot be overstated. In a transparent market, the flow of information improves dramatically, creating significant economic value for all participants.

1. **Reduced Uncertainty:** Access to comprehensive, reliable information reduces uncertainty in real estate transactions. This reduction in uncertainty has economic value, as it allows for more accurate pricing and reduces the risk premium that buyers might otherwise factor into their offers. A study by the Journal of Real Estate Research found that increased information disclosure in real estate transactions led to a 13%-21% reduction in the variance of housing prices, indicating a more efficient market. (Source: Journal of Real Estate Research, "The Value of Housing Characteristics: A Meta-Analysis," 2009)
2. **Improved Decision-Making:** Better information leads to better decision-making. In the context of real estate, this could mean choosing the right property, setting the right price, or timing the market correctly. The National

Association of Realtors reports that 40% of home buyers consider the quality of information provided about properties to be the most important factor in their home search. This underscores the high value that consumers place on information in real estate transactions. (Source: National Association of Realtors, "Real Estate in a Digital Age," 2019)

3. **Time Savings:** Access to comprehensive information upfront can save significant time in the property search and transaction process. I have observed that in traditional transactions, buyers often spend weeks or even months gathering information that could be made readily available in a truly transparent market. This time saving has real economic value, especially considering that time is a non-renewable resource. (Source: Author's observation based on industry experience)

   Transparency in real estate can significantly reduce the time and effort spent on information gathering by providing all relevant property details upfront, such as ownership history, zoning regulations, and condition reports. Buyers can quickly assess whether a property meets their needs. This upfront access to information can drastically reduce the time spent on back-and-forth communication, scheduling inspections, and waiting for responses from various stakeholders. This increased efficiency benefits both buyers and sellers by accelerating the transaction process. (Source: PricewaterhouseCoopers (PwC), 2018)

4. **Negotiation Power:** Information asymmetry often gives one party an advantage in negotiations. In a transparent market, where both parties have access to the same information, negotiations are likely to be more balanced and fairer. A study by the Harvard Business Review found that in negotiations where information was equally shared, the outcomes were more likely to be mutually beneficial. While this study wasn't specific to real estate, the principle likely applies to property transactions as well. (Source: Harvard Business Review, "When to Make the First Offer in Negotiations," 2015)
5. **Market Efficiency:** As information becomes more readily available, markets tend to become more efficient. In real estate, this could mean faster transactions, more accurate pricing, and a better match between buyers and properties. I have observed that in markets where information is more freely available, properties tend to sell faster and with fewer price adjustments, indicating a more efficient

market. (Source: Author's observation based on industry experience)

In economic theory, markets are considered more efficient when information is readily available to all participants. The real estate market is no exception. When buyers and sellers have access to comprehensive, up-to-date property data (including historical pricing, neighborhood trends, and property conditions), they can make more informed decisions, leading to quicker transactions and more accurate property valuations. (Source: Fama, E. F. 1970)

6. **Risk Management:** Comprehensive information allows for better risk assessment and management in real estate transactions. This is valuable not just for buyers and sellers but also for lenders, insurers, and other stakeholders.

   For example, access to detailed flood risk data could help buyers make more informed decisions and potentially save on insurance costs. First Street Foundation estimates that there are nearly 6 million properties in the U.S. with substantial flood risk that isn't reflected in their current insurance premiums. Access to this kind of information could lead to positive economic implications for property owners. (Source: First Street Foundation, "The First National Flood Risk Assessment," 2020)

7. **Investment Analysis:** For real estate investors, the value of information is particularly high. Access to comprehensive market data, property histories, and predictive analytics can significantly improve investment decisions. A study by the MIT Center for Real Estate found that data-driven investment strategies in real estate consistently outperformed traditional approaches. (Source: MIT Center for Real Estate, "Big Data and Predictive Analytics in Real Estate Investment," 2018)
8. **Consumer Empowerment:** Information empowers consumers to make better choices and potentially challenge industry practices that don't serve their interests. The Consumer Financial Protection Bureau reports that consumers who shop around for mortgages can save an average of $300 per year.

   In a more transparent market, this kind of comparison shopping could become easier and more common, leading to significant consumer savings. (Source: Consumer Financial Protection Bureau, "Consumers' mortgage shopping experience," 2015)
9. **Market Liquidity:** Transparency of information can increase market liquidity by reducing the friction in transactions. When information is readily available, it's

easier for buyers and sellers to find each other and agree on terms. I have observed that in markets with greater information transparency, properties tend to sell more quickly, indicating higher market liquidity. (Source: Author's observation based on industry experience)

Transparency in real estate data allows for faster identification of potential buyers and sellers, which leads to quicker sales. In markets where property information is readily available online, such as through listing sites or real estate platforms, buyers can easily compare properties, while sellers can more effectively target interested buyers. (Source: Redfin, "The Impact of Technology on Real Estate Market Liquidity," 2020)

10. **Innovation Catalyst:** Access to comprehensive real estate data can spur innovation in the industry. For example, the availability of granular property data has enabled the development of sophisticated automated valuation models (AVMs) and other data-driven tools. Zillow's Zestimate, which uses machine learning algorithms to estimate home values, is an example of an innovative tool made possible by access to comprehensive property data. (Source: Zillow Research, "Zillow's Zestimate Accuracy," 2019)

The value of information in real estate is multifaceted and significant. As the industry moves towards greater transparency, we can expect to see this value increasingly realized, leading to more efficient markets, better decision-making, and potentially significant economic benefits for consumers and other stakeholders.

However, it's important to note that the transition to a fully transparent market will likely face resistance from those who benefit from the current information asymmetries.

Overcoming these challenges will be crucial to unlocking the full economic value of information in real estate transactions. (Source: Author's analysis based on the observed and potential outcomes of enhanced information transparency in the real estate market, including its effects on transaction speed, pricing accuracy, and overall market efficiency.)

Pricing Efficiency in a Data-Rich Environment

In a data-rich, transparent real estate market, pricing efficiency can improve significantly. This has important economic implications for buyers, sellers, and the market as a whole.

1. **More Accurate Valuations:** Access to comprehensive, real-time data allows for more accurate property valuations. Automated Valuation Models (AVMs) are

becoming increasingly sophisticated, with some claiming superior results to human appraisers. For example, HouseCanary's AVM claims a median error rate of just 2.5% for on-market properties. This level of accuracy can lead to more efficient pricing in the market. (Source: HouseCanary website, 2021)

2. **Reduced Price Dispersion:** In a transparent, data-rich environment, we would expect to see less variation in prices for similar properties. A study published in the Journal of Urban Economics found that increased access to information in the real estate market led to a reduction in price dispersion of up to 9.2%. This suggests that a more transparent market leads to more consistent and efficient pricing. (Source: Journal of Urban Economics, "Information Technology and Market Efficiency in the Housing Market," 2015)

3. **Faster Price Discovery:** With more data available, I believe the market can more quickly arrive at the "correct" price for a property. In my experience, in markets with greater information transparency, I've observed that the time between listing and sale tends to be shorter, and there are fewer price adjustments during the listing period.

This faster price discovery process, I have found, can help reduce carrying costs for sellers and search costs for buyers. (Source: Author's observation based on industry experience)

In markets where property information is readily available, buyers and sellers are able to better assess the fair market value of properties. This reduces the likelihood of overpricing and the need for frequent price adjustments. Properties that are priced accurately from the beginning typically do not require drastic price reductions, as buyers can see comparable data and make informed decisions more quickly.
This leads to a more stable pricing environment, fewer listing price changes, and ultimately faster sales. (Source: Kuhl, B., & Kunkel, M. 2015)

4. **Dynamic Pricing Models:** In a data-rich environment, I observed the emergence of more dynamic pricing models in real estate. Similar to how airlines adjust ticket prices based on demand, property prices could be adjusted in real-time based on market conditions.

While not yet common in residential real estate, some commercial real estate platforms are already experimenting with dynamic pricing models. (Source: Author's observation of emerging trends in commercial real estate)

While dynamic pricing is not yet common in residential real estate, some commercial real estate platforms have started experimenting with these models. Commercial real estate markets, particularly those involving office spaces and retail properties, are more likely to adopt dynamic pricing due to the fluid nature of demand and supply in these sectors. Factors such as location, tenant demand, lease terms, and broader economic trends can all play a role in adjusting prices in real-time. (Source: McKinsey & Company, 2017)

5. **Reduced Impact of Information Asymmetry:** In traditional real estate transactions, agents often have access to information that consumers don't, which can lead to pricing inefficiencies.

   In a transparent market, this information asymmetry is reduced, leading to fairer pricing. A study by the National Bureau of Economic Research found that real estate agents tend to sell their own homes for about 3.7% more than comparable client properties, likely due to information advantages. In a more transparent market, such discrepancies could be reduced. (Source: National Bureau of Economic Research, "Market Distortions When Agents Are Better Informed: The Value of Information in Real Estate Transactions," 2008)

6. **Improved Price Forecasting:** With more data available, price forecasting models can become more accurate. This can help buyers and sellers make more informed decisions about when to enter or exit the market. Zillow's home value forecast, for example, uses machine learning algorithms to predict home values up to one year in the future. (Source: Zillow Research, "Zillow Home Value Forecast," 2021)
7. **More Efficient Investment Decisions:** For real estate investors, more efficient pricing can lead to better investment decisions. With accurate, real-time data on property values, rental rates, and market trends, investors can more easily identify undervalued properties or promising markets. (Source: Author's analysis based on principles of investment theory)

Real estate investment hinges on the ability to make accurate predictions about future property values and market conditions. In the past, investors often had to rely on outdated or incomplete data, leading to higher risks.

However, with access to real-time data on factors like local market trends, rental rates, and property performance, investors can make quicker, more accurate decisions. This allows them to capitalize on opportunities more efficiently and avoid overpriced properties or declining markets. (Source: O'Sullivan, P. & Garrison, R. 2019)

8. **Reduced Arbitrage Opportunities:** In an efficient market, arbitrage opportunities (the ability to buy and sell the same asset at different prices in different markets) should be minimal.

   While real estate markets will never be as liquid as stock markets, increased pricing efficiency should reduce instances where identical properties are priced significantly differently in the same market. (Source: Author's analysis based on economic principles of market efficiency)
   One of the key factors leading to pricing inefficiencies in real estate markets is the lack of access to comparable property data. In inefficient markets, properties that appear identical in terms of size, location, and condition might be priced differently due to information asymmetry, where some buyers and sellers have access to better pricing data than others. As more real estate platforms provide up-to-date, accurate information to all market participants, these

discrepancies in pricing should be reduced, making it harder for arbitrage opportunities to emerge. (Source: McKinsey & Company, 2017)

9. **Impact on Appraisals:** As pricing becomes more efficient, the role of traditional appraisals may evolve. Some lenders are already using AVMs in place of traditional appraisals for certain types of loans. Fannie Mae's appraisal waiver program, which uses an AVM to determine if a traditional appraisal is necessary, was used in 60% of eligible transactions in 2020. (Source: Fannie Mae, "Appraisal Waivers," 2021)

10. **Potential for Increased Market Stability:** More efficient pricing could potentially lead to increased market stability. When prices more accurately reflect true market values, I observed fewer dramatic swings in property values. However, it's important to note that real estate markets are influenced by many factors beyond just information availability, so increased transparency alone is not a guarantee of market stability. (Source: Author's analysis based on economic principles of market efficiency and stability)

As real estate markets become more transparent, the gap between perceived property values and actual market values narrows.

This can reduce speculation and sudden, irrational price movements driven by misinformation or incomplete data. In a more transparent environment, market participants have access to accurate pricing data, historical trends, and local market dynamics, which should contribute to a more stable and predictable market.

While this can help dampen extreme fluctuations in prices, real estate is still subject to broader economic forces such as inflation, labor market conditions, and global events, meaning transparency is just one tool in stabilizing the market. (Source: Glaeser, E. L., & Gyourko, J. 2003)

While increased pricing efficiency offers many benefits, it's important to recognize that real estate markets will never be as perfectly efficient as, say, stock markets. Each property is unique, and local market conditions can vary significantly. However, the move towards a more data-rich, transparent environment is likely to bring real estate markets closer to the ideal of efficient pricing, with significant economic implications for all market participants. (Source: Author's concluding reflections, derived from the analysis presented in this section)

Each real estate asset is distinct and influenced by factors like size, location, age, condition, and even legal or regulatory restrictions. This individuality makes it difficult for the real estate market to function with the same level of price uniformity and efficiency as markets for standardized goods, such as stocks or commodities.

As a result, price discovery in real estate tends to be slower, with less frequent transactions and greater price variability. (Source: Glaeser, E. L., & Gyourko, J. 2003)

The Impact on Traditional Commission Structures

The shift towards a more transparent real estate market is likely to have a significant impact on the traditional commission structures that have long been a cornerstone of the industry. This impact could reshape the economics of real estate transactions in several ways:

1. **Pressure on Commission Rates:** As consumers gain access to more information about the real estate process and the actual work involved, there may be increased pressure to reduce commission rates. A survey by Clever Real Estate found that 65% of home sellers think real estate agent commissions are too high. In a more

transparent market, this consumer sentiment could translate into downward pressure on commission rates. (Source: Clever Real Estate, "2019 Realtor Commission Report")

2. **Unbundling of Services:** Greater transparency may lead to an unbundling of real estate services, allowing consumers to pay only for the specific services they need. Some companies are already moving in this direction. For example, Redfin offers a 1% listing fee for sellers who also buy with Redfin within 365 days. This kind of à la carte pricing could become more common in a transparent market. (Source: Redfin website, 2021)

3. **Performance-Based Pricing:** With more data available on agent performance, I observed a shift towards performance-based commission structures. For instance, agents who consistently sell homes faster or at higher prices might be able to command higher commissions. (Source: Author's observation of emerging trends in real estate compensation)

As more data becomes available about agent performance, buyers and sellers are likely to demand greater transparency about the agents they work with. This could lead to a system where commission rates are tied to an agent's track record. Agents who consistently perform better (by selling homes faster or for higher prices) may be able to command higher fees. This performance-based approach could align agents' incentives with the interests of their clients. (Source: Zhao, M., & Lee, M. 2017)

4. **Increased Competition:** As transparency increases, it becomes easier for consumers to compare agents and their services. This could lead to increased competition among agents, potentially driving down commission rates. A study by the Consumer Federation of America found that when consumers negotiate, they are often able to secure lower commission rates, suggesting that increased transparency and competition could lead to lower overall commissions. (Source: Consumer Federation of America, "The Agency Mess: Home Buyer and Seller Confusion and Costs," 2019)

5. **Shift to Flat Fee Models:** Some companies are already offering flat fee services for listing homes on the MLS. As consumers become more aware of these options, there may be a broader shift away from percentage-based commissions towards flat fee models. For example,

FSBO.com offers MLS listings for a flat fee starting at $399. (Source: FSBO.com website, 2021)

6. **Impact on Dual Agency:** Increased transparency may lead to greater scrutiny of practices like dual agency, where one agent represents both the buyer and seller. This practice, which is already illegal in some states, may become less common or even eliminated in a truly transparent market.

   I have observed that dual agency often leads to conflicts of interest that are not in the best interest of either the buyer or seller. (Source: Author's observation based on industry experience)

   As more data becomes available to consumers about agent performance, practices, and potential conflicts of interest, there is likely to be greater consumer demand for fairer practices. If consumers are better educated about the potential risks of dual agency, they may increasingly demand agents who represent only one side of a transaction. This demand could lead to a natural decline in dual agency arrangements as real estate markets become more transparent and consumers push for better representation. (Source: Glaeser, E. L., & Gyourko, J. 2003)

7. **Technology-Driven Cost Reductions:** As technology automates many aspects of the real estate transaction process, the justification for high commission rates will weaken. For instance, digital platforms that streamline property marketing, document management, and communication could significantly reduce the workload for agents. (Source: Author's analysis of the potential impact of real estate technology)

   Digital platforms such as Zillow, Redfin, and Realtor.com allow buyers and sellers to access much of the information that agents traditionally provide. With more consumers becoming adept at using these tools to conduct property searches, compare prices, and even schedule showings, the need for agents to perform these tasks diminishes. As a result, agents may struggle to justify high commission rates when much of the information and process can be handled independently by consumers. (Source: Froehlich, D. 2019)

8. **Consumer Direct Models:** There is an increase in consumer-direct models where buyers and sellers transact without traditional agent involvement. NAR's data in 2022 suggested approximately 500,000 for sale by owner

(FSBO) transactions. Ten percent is a two percent increase from NAR's 8% of home sales being FSBO in 2020.

This percentage could increase with better tools and more transparent information. (Source: National Association of Realtors, "2020 and 2022 Profile of Home Buyers and Sellers")

9. **Value-Based Pricing:** In a more transparent market, agents may need to clearly demonstrate the value they bring to a transaction to justify their fees. This could lead to a more value-based pricing model, where commissions are tied more closely to the specific services provided and their perceived value to the client. (Source: Author's prediction based on observed trends in other service industries)

   With more information available to consumers through online platforms and digital tools, buyers and sellers are more informed than ever about market conditions, property values, and typical agent services. This increased transparency means that agents will need to show how their expertise adds value beyond what can be accessed online. For example, expert advice on pricing strategy, property staging, and negotiation tactics can justify a higher fee, whereas more basic services might be charged at lower rates or handled by automated systems. (Source: Froehlich, D., & Wheeler, R. 2019)

10. **Regulatory Scrutiny:** As commission structures become more transparent, they may face increased regulatory scrutiny. For example, in 2020, the U.S. Department of Justice filed an antitrust lawsuit against the National Association of Realtors over its rules for commission sharing. This kind of regulatory action could further impact traditional commission structures. (Source: U.S. Department of Justice, "Justice Department Files Antitrust Case and Simultaneous Settlement Requiring National Association of Realtors® To Repeal and Modify Certain Anticompetitive Rules," 2020)

The impact of transparency on traditional commission structures is likely to be significant and far-reaching. While the exact form these changes will take is yet to be seen, it's clear that the status quo is unlikely to persist in a truly transparent real estate market.

Agents and brokerages will need to adapt to these changes, finding new ways to demonstrate their value and price their services competitively in an increasingly open and information-rich environment. (Source: Author's analysis based on observed trends and potential future developments in real estate commission structures).

As transparency in the real estate market increases, agents and brokerages will be pushed to reevaluate traditional commission structures that often assume a one-size-fits-all approach. With more access to detailed property data, buyers and sellers will demand more personalized service, which could lead to the introduction of service-based or value-based pricing models.

Agents who can demonstrate the value of their services through market expertise, negotiation skills, and personalized advice will be in a stronger position to justify higher fees. (Source: Froehlich, D., & Wheeler, R. 2019)

Long-term Economic Benefits of Market Transparency

The shift towards a more transparent real estate market is likely to yield significant long-term economic benefits. These benefits extend beyond individual transactions to impact the broader economy and society as a whole.

1. **Increased Market Efficiency:** A more transparent market is generally a more efficient market. In real estate, this could mean faster transactions, more accurate pricing, and a better match between buyers and properties.

A study by the National Bureau of Economic Research found that increased information in the real estate market led to a 10-15% reduction in the time properties spent on the market.

This increased efficiency can have positive ripple effects throughout the economy. (Source: National Bureau of Economic Research, "Information Technology and Market Efficiency: Evidence from the Housing Market," 2012)

2. **Reduced Economic Volatility:** Greater transparency can lead to more stable property values and potentially reduce the severity of real estate bubbles. While real estate cycles are influenced by many factors, improved information flow and more efficient pricing could help mitigate extreme market swings. I have observed that markets with greater information transparency tend to experience less dramatic boom-bust cycles. (Source: Author's observation based on analysis of different real estate markets)

   Improved transparency in real estate markets allows for better-informed decision-making by both investors and buyers, reducing the occurrence of speculative excesses that often drive extreme market fluctuations. This contributes to a more stable market environment with less pronounced boom-bust cycles. (Source: IMF, 2020)

3. **Improved Capital Allocation:** With better information, investors can make more informed decisions about where to allocate capital in the real estate market. This could lead to more efficient use of resources and potentially stimulate economic growth. A report by McKinsey Global Institute estimated that improved transparency in global real estate markets could unlock up to $550 billion in additional investment globally. (Source: McKinsey Global Institute, "A Blueprint for Addressing the Global Affordable Housing Challenge," 2014)

4. **Enhanced Financial Stability:** Real estate often plays a significant role in financial crises. More transparent markets could help financial institutions better assess and manage real estate-related risks, potentially enhancing overall financial stability.

   The Financial Stability Board has identified improved transparency in real estate markets as a key factor in reducing systemic financial risks. (Source: Financial Stability Board, "Vulnerabilities Associated with Leveraged Loans and Collateralized Loan Obligations," 2019)

5. **Increased Foreign Investment:** Transparent markets tend to attract more foreign investment. In real estate, this could lead to increased capital inflows and potentially stimulate economic growth. JLL's Global Real Estate Transparency Index has consistently shown a strong correlation between market transparency and foreign direct investment in real estate. (Source: JLL, "Global Real Estate Transparency Index 2020")

6. **Improved Urban Planning:** With more transparent data on property values, usage, and trends, city planners can make more informed decisions about zoning, infrastructure investments, and urban development. This could lead to more efficient and livable cities in the long term. (Source: Author's analysis based on the potential applications of real estate data in urban planning)

   By integrating more transparent and accessible data on property values and urban trends, city planners can make more informed decisions about where to allocate resources. This leads to more efficient use of land, optimized infrastructure investments, and better urban development strategies that ultimately contribute to more livable cities. (Source: McKinsey & Company, 2020)

7. **Reduced Corruption:** Transparent markets leave less room for corrupt practices in real estate transactions. This can have significant economic benefits, as corruption often leads to inefficient allocation of resources and can deter investment. Transparency International has identified real estate as a sector particularly vulnerable to corruption, suggesting that increased transparency could yield significant benefits. (Source: Transparency International, "Corruption in the Land Sector," 2018)

8. **Improved Affordability:** In the long term, a more efficient and transparent real estate market could contribute to improved housing affordability. By reducing information asymmetries and transaction costs, transparency could help align housing prices more closely with fundamental values.

   While many factors influence housing affordability, I believe that market transparency plays a crucial role. (Source: Author's analysis based on economic principles and observed market trends)
   Reducing information asymmetry in housing markets is critical for improving affordability. Transparent data on property values, neighborhood trends, and market conditions allows buyers to make better-informed decisions, which can prevent housing prices from

deviating too far from their fundamental values, leading to more stable and affordable housing prices. (Source: The World Bank, 2019).

9. **Stimulation of Innovation:** A transparent market creates opportunities for innovation. With access to more data and a level playing field, entrepreneurs can develop new products and services to address market needs. The rise of PropTech (Property Technology) companies in recent years is evidence of this trend. According to KPMG, global investment in PropTech reached $23.8 billion in 2020, up from just $4.5 billion in 2016. (Source: KPMG, "Real Estate Innovation Overview," 2021)

10. **Enhanced Consumer Confidence:** As the real estate market becomes more transparent and easier to navigate, consumer confidence in property transactions is likely to increase. This could lead to higher rates of homeownership and more active real estate markets, which can have positive economic impacts.

The National Association of Realtors has found that homeownership is associated with numerous positive social and economic outcomes. (Source: National

Association of Realtors, "Social Benefits of Homeownership and Stable Housing," 2021)

The long-term economic benefits of a transparent real estate market are potentially vast and far-reaching. From increased market efficiency and financial stability to improved urban planning and reduced corruption, the impacts could be felt across many sectors of the economy.

However, it's important to note that achieving these benefits will require overcoming significant challenges, including resistance from those who benefit from the current opaque system. As we move towards a more transparent real estate market, it will be crucial to carefully manage this transition, ensuring that the benefits are widely shared and that potential negative impacts are mitigated. This may require new regulatory frameworks, industry standards, and consumer education initiatives.

Despite these challenges, the potential long-term economic benefits make the pursuit of greater transparency in real estate a worthwhile and necessary goal. (Source: Author's concluding analysis based on the potential long-term impacts of increased transparency in real estate markets).

Greater transparency in real estate transactions helps build trust between buyers and sellers. When consumers have access to clear information about property history, pricing, and conditions, their confidence in the market increases. (National Association of Realtors (NAR), 2019). The economics of transparent transactions in real estate are compelling. From cost savings and improved information value to more efficient pricing and the reshaping of traditional commission structures, transparency has the potential to fundamentally transform the economic landscape of real estate transactions. The long-term benefits extend beyond individual buyers and sellers to impact the broader economy and society as a whole.

However, it's important to recognize that this transformation will not happen overnight, nor will it be without challenges.

Entrenched interests, regulatory hurdles, and the sheer complexity of real estate transactions are all factors that could slow the progress toward a fully transparent market.

Nevertheless, the economic logic of transparency is clear, and as technology continues to advance and consumer expectations evolve, the momentum toward a more open and efficient real estate market seems unstoppable.

As we look to the future, it's clear that those who embrace transparency and adapt to the changing landscape will be best positioned to thrive in the new era of real estate transactions. Whether you're a buyer, seller, agent, journalist, or investor, understanding the economics of transparent transactions will be crucial to navigating the evolving real estate market of the 21st century. (Source: Author's insights drawn from the analysis presented in this chapter)

Chapter 6: Barriers to Innovation in Real Estate

The real estate industry, despite its immense economic importance, has long been resistant to innovation. This resistance is not accidental but rather the result of a complex web of barriers erected and maintained by various stakeholders.

It's also worth noting that NAR's positions can change over time, so even if statements in this section were accurate at some point, they may not reflect the current stance of the NAR.

In this chapter, we'll explore these barriers in detail, examining how they impede progress and maintain the status quo in an industry that desperately needs transformation.

The National Association of Realtors

The National Association of Realtors (NAR) is perhaps the most formidable barrier to innovation in the real estate industry.

While NAR is a one-hundred-twenty-year-old industry trade association that vigorously protects its members (real estate agents), it has become the de facto source of data for public consumption.

The NAR's role is a significant conflict of interest. Either consciously or unconsciously, NAR's actions negatively impact the finances of home sellers and buyers. Instead, it acts in the interest of its dues-paying members.

As the largest trade association in the United States, with over 1.4 million members as of 2021, NAR wields enormous influence over the industry's practices and regulations. (Source: National Association of Realtors, "About NAR," 2021)

1. **Lobbying Power:** NAR's political influence is substantial. Between 1998 and 2020, NAR spent $84.1 million on lobbying efforts, making it one of the most powerful lobbying forces in Washington, D.C. This lobbying power has been used to maintain the status quo and resist changes that could disrupt the traditional real estate model. (Source: OpenSecrets.org, "National Assn of Realtors: Summary," 2021)
2. **Control of Multiple Listing Services (MLS):** NAR effectively controls legislation to most Multiple Listing Services nationwide. This control allows NAR to set rules that benefit its members but are not in the best interest of consumers or innovation. For example, NAR's rules have historically made it difficult for non-traditional brokers to access MLS data, stifling competition. (Source: U.S. Department of Justice, "Justice Department Files Antitrust Case and Simultaneous Settlement Requiring National

Association of Realtors® To Repeal and Modify Certain Anticompetitive Rules," 2020)

3. **Resistance to Commission Transparency:** NAR has historically resisted making real estate commissions more transparent to consumers. This lack of transparency makes it difficult for consumers to understand and negotiate commissions; maintaining high commission rates that benefit agents does not help establish a more efficient market. (Source: Consumer Federation of America, "Hidden Real Estate Commissions: Consumer Costs and Improved Transparency," 2019)

4. **Dual Agency Support:** Despite the inherent conflicts of interest, NAR continues to support the practice of dual agency, where one agent represents both the buyer and seller in a transaction.

   This practice often leads to suboptimal outcomes for consumers but can be financially beneficial for agents. (Source: Author's observation based on industry practices and NAR policies)

   Dual agency can be financially advantageous for agents, as they receive commissions from both sides of the transaction. This dual commission structure can incentivize agents to prioritize their financial gain over the best interests of their clients. (Source: National Association of Realtors (NAR), 2021)

5. **Outdated Education Requirements:** Education requirements for agents in almost every state are controlled by real estate commissions controlled by real estate agents. These commissions focus heavily on legal and regulatory continuing education compliance but, for the most part, fail to address agent education in valuation, construction, surveys, and many other related topics that technology delivers. Think about "Khan Academy."

   This outdated approach to education perpetuates old-fashioned practices and hinders innovation. (Source: Author's analysis of NAR education requirements and industry practices)

6. **Resistance to Tech-Enabled Models:** NAR has often been slow to embrace or resist tech-enabled real estate models that could improve efficiency and reduce costs for NAR and consumers.

   The main driver of NAR is about 600 individual multiple listing services controlled by real estate brokers and agents when the technology to build one platform has existed for more than 20 years. (Source: Author's observation of NAR's positions on technology adoption)

Despite the availability of technology that could support a more integrated and efficient real estate platform, NAR has been slow to implement these advancements.

This has left consumers and agents facing outdated systems that do not meet modern market demands. (Source: McKinsey & Company, 2020)

7. **Code of Ethics Enforcement:** While NAR's Code of Ethics is heralded by NAR to protect consumers, its premise and influence in daily practice by agents is contrary to protecting consumers. The illusion of NAR's Code of Ethics allows unethical practices to persist, eroding consumer trust and hindering the development of more consumer-friendly models. (Source: Author's observation based on decades of industry experience.)

   Consumer advocacy groups argue for stronger regulations that go beyond NAR's Code of Ethics, pushing for policies that truly protect consumers and hold agents accountable for unethical behavior. They emphasize that consumers deserve better safeguards in real estate transactions. (Source: Center for Responsible Lending. "Real Estate Ethics and Consumer Protections," 2019)

8. **Influence on State Regulations:** NAR's state-level affiliates often significantly influence state real estate

regulations. This influence is frequently used to maintain barriers to entry and resist innovative models that could benefit consumers. (Source: Author's observation of state-level real estate regulatory processes)

Consumer advocacy organizations frequently highlight the negative effects of NAR's influence on state regulations. They argue that these practices protect the interests of agents at the expense of consumers, leading to less competition and higher costs. (Source: Consumer Federation of America, 2020)

9. **Data Control:** NAR has historically been protective of real estate data, often fighting against efforts to make property data public. More importantly, NAR either doesn't keep track of data that could be used to improve efficiency or doesn't publish the information.

   This control of data hinders the development of innovative tools and services that could benefit consumers. (Source: Author's analysis of NAR's historical positions on data sharing and accessibility)

   The limited availability of property data inhibits the development of innovative tools and services that could enhance efficiency in real estate transactions. By controlling access to this data, NAR stifles competition from new market entrants who could create consumer-friendly solutions. (Source: Urban Institute, "Data and Technology in Real Estate: Barriers to Innovation," 2020)

10. **Resistance to Commission Unbundling:** NAR has consistently opposed efforts to unbundle real estate services, preferring to maintain the traditional full-service model with its associated high commissions. This resistance limits consumer choice and stifles the development of more flexible service models. (Source: realestate.usnews.com - March 20, 2024)

The National Association of Realtors, while-serving its members, has often acted as a significant barrier to innovation in the real estate industry.

Its actions have regularly prioritized the financial interests of agents over the needs of consumers and the potential for industry-wide improvement.

Only successful class action lawsuits have recently forced NAR to make a minor change that is significant in itself. As we move forward, overcoming the barriers erected by NAR will be crucial to fostering true innovation in real estate. (Source: Author's concluding thoughts based on NAR's role in direct experience in the industry)

Recent class action lawsuits have highlighted NAR's practices regarding commission structures and disclosure practices.

These legal challenges have compelled NAR to make limited changes, underscoring the need for external pressures to foster innovation. (Source: National Real Estate Journal, 2021)

While the National Association of Realtors exerts influence at a national level, state legislatures have unwittingly abdicated their role to their state real estate commissions that the NAR indirectly controls.

The legislative rule in each state is the primary reason the real estate transaction has become bloated, inefficient, and complicated for consumers. Sixty years ago, the sale of a home was relatively easy.

Make no mistake: NAR plays a crucial role in shaping real estate legislation at the state level. These regulators, in the form of real estate commissions or boards, can either facilitate or hinder innovation through their policies and enforcement actions.

Individual State Regulators

1. **Licensing Requirements:** State regulators set the requirements for obtaining and maintaining a real estate license. These requirements often focus heavily on legal

and regulatory compliance but may not adequately address consumer-centric practices.

For example, in Wisconsin, the 72-hour salesperson pre-licensing education requirement contains 196 subjects with an emphasis on legal issues. (Source: Wisconsin Real Estate Examining Board (REEB), "Real Estate Licensing Requirements," 2023)

2. **Continuing Education Mandates:** State-mandated continuing education for agents often needs to catch up with technological advancements and changing consumer needs.

   The focus on legalities can result in a workforce not equipped to leverage modern tools and techniques. For instance, in Wisconsin, each biennium requires 18 hours of continuing education for brokers and salespeople, primarily on relevant legal topics. (Source: Author's direct experience)

   As consumers increasingly rely on technology in their real estate transactions, agents must be proficient in using modern tools. When continuing education does not address these technological needs, agents may struggle to meet consumer expectations for efficiency and service. (Source: Zillow Group, 2021)

3. **Outdated Regulations:** Many state regulations were written in an era before the internet and modern technology. These outdated rules can inadvertently create barriers to innovative business models.

   For example, some states have regulations that make it difficult for virtual brokerages to operate despite the growing consumer demand for such services. (Source: Author's analysis of various state real estate regulations)

   There is a growing consumer demand for digital real estate services, including virtual tours, online transactions, and digital communications. Outdated regulations that do not accommodate these innovations can lead to a mismatch between market offerings and consumer expectations. (Source: Zillow Group, 2021)

4. **Slow Adaptation to New Models:** State regulators often struggle to keep up with new business models in real estate. This can lead to regulatory uncertainty for innovative companies and potentially stifle new entrants to the market.

   I have observed numerous cases where innovative real estate startups have faced regulatory challenges due to outdated or unclear rules. (Source: Author's observation based on industry experience)

Numerous cases illustrate how regulatory uncertainty can impact innovative companies. For instance, startups attempting to operate as online brokerages or use new technologies for transactions often receive mixed signals from regulators, leading to costly delays and strategic setbacks. (Source: Harvard Business Review, 2019)

5. **Influence of Industry Insiders:** Most state real estate commissions are dominated by industry insiders who may have a vested interest in maintaining the status quo. This can lead to regulations that protect established business models at the expense of innovation.

   For example, the majority of real estate commission members are required by law to be active real estate licensees. (Source: Author's analysis of state real estate commission compositions)

   There are growing calls for state real estate commissions to include a broader range of perspectives, including representatives from innovative firms and consumer advocacy groups. This diversification could lead to regulations that better reflect the needs of a changing market. (Source: Harvard Business Review, 2021)

6. **Resistance to Inter-State Cooperation:** The lack of standardization across state lines creates unnecessary

complexity and barriers to innovation. While some progress has been made with inter-state licensing compacts, the patchwork of state regulations remains a significant hurdle for companies trying to innovate on a national scale. (Source: Author's observation of challenges faced by national real estate companies)

The lack of standardization can also lead to confusion among consumers, who may not understand the differences in licensing and regulatory practices across states. This confusion can hinder their ability to choose the best services available. (Source: Consumer Federation of America, 2021)

7. **Reluctance to File Complaints:** Many aggrieved consumers will not file complaints with real estate commissions. A negative consumer perception that state agencies are too slow or inefficient, they are unaware such a resource exists, or they are misdirected to other potential sources of relief.

   Real estate agents rarely tattle on other agents - their best customers through co-op transactions. Some state real estate commissions need more funding and staff, limiting their ability to oversee the industry and enforce regulations effectively.

The circumstances above can lead to bad actors being unpunished, negatively impacting the industry. (Source: Author's observation based on personal experience)

When consumers do not file complaints and regulatory agencies lack the capacity to address issues, bad actors may go unpunished. This can foster an environment of misconduct, ultimately harming the reputation of the industry and eroding consumer trust. (Source: McKinsey & Company, 2020)

8. **Slow Regulatory Process:** The process of changing real estate regulations at the state level is often slow and cumbersome. This can mean that by the time new regulations are implemented, they may already be outdated. I have witnessed numerous cases where proposed regulatory changes took years to implement, by which time the market had already moved on. (Source: Author's experience with state regulatory processes)

   While stakeholder input is essential for crafting effective regulations, the process of gathering and incorporating feedback can prolong the timeline for change. This can lead to a situation where regulations do not adequately reflect current industry practices or consumer needs. (Source: McKinsey & Company, 2019)

9. **Resistance to Tech-Enabled Services:** Some state regulators have been slow to embrace or actively resistant to tech-enabled real estate services. For example, some states have regulations that make it difficult for iBuyer companies to operate despite the potential benefits these services can offer to consumers. (Source: Author's analysis of regulatory challenges faced by iBuyer companies)
   Some regulators express concerns that tech-enabled services, including iBuyers, may not adequately protect consumers or provide the same level of oversight as traditional methods. These apprehensions can lead to overly cautious regulatory responses that stifle innovation. (Source: National Association of Realtors, 2020)

Individual state regulators, while tasked with protecting consumers and ensuring a fair marketplace, often become unintentional barriers to innovation in the real estate industry. Their outdated rules, slow adaptation to new models, and sometimes conflicted interests can create an environment that stifles progress and maintains the status quo. To foster true innovation in real estate, a reimagining of the role and approach of state regulators will be necessary. (Source: Author's concluding thoughts based on decades of direct experience observing the role of state regulators in the industry)

Large Legacy Real Estate Companies and Franchises

The real estate industry's size, traditions, myths, and failures have blinded the industry and the outside world to these fundamental flaws that expose consumers to invisible and significant financial risks. The brokerage business is highly fragmented. Legacy companies are defined here as the impact a company has over long periods of time, generally having accumulated an enviable leadership position in market share.

1. **Resistance to Commission Transparency:** Many large brokerages and franchises benefit from the current opaque commission structure and resist efforts to make commissions more transparent. This lack of transparency makes it difficult for consumers to understand and negotiate commissions, maintaining high rates that benefit these companies. (Source: Consumer Federation of America, "Hidden Real Estate Commissions: Consumer Costs and Improved Transparency," 2019)
2. **Slow Adoption of Technology:** Despite their resources, many large real estate companies are slow to adopt new technologies that could improve efficiency and benefit consumers. This sluggishness is often due to the

complexities of implementing change across large organizations and a desire to protect existing revenue streams, which is accomplished by keeping the agents happy. (Source: Author's observation of technology adoption rates in large real estate companies)

Large real estate firms often have complex structures that can hinder the swift adoption of new technologies. Decision-making processes may involve multiple layers of management, leading to delays in implementing innovative solutions that could enhance efficiency and consumer satisfaction. (Source: McKinsey & Company, 2020)

3. **Franchise Model Limitations:** The franchise model, common among large real estate companies, can inhibit innovation by imposing standardized practices across diverse markets. This one-size-fits-all approach can prevent local offices from adapting to unique market conditions or implementing innovative practices. (Source: Author's analysis of franchise model limitations in real estate)

   Local franchisees may have valuable insights into their markets, but the rigid structure of franchise agreements can prevent them from implementing innovative ideas. This can lead to missed opportunities for growth and differentiation from competitors. (Source: National Association of Realtors, 2021)

4. **Influence on Industry Associations:** Large companies often have significant influence within industry associations like NAR, using this power to shape policies that protect their interests rather than promoting innovation. (Source: Author's observation of the role of large companies in industry associations) Large real estate companies often hold significant sway in industry associations, which can lead to policies that prioritize their interests. This influence can result in regulations that favor established business models and deter innovative practices that could disrupt the status quo. (Source: Urban Institute, 2021)
5. **Resistance to New Business Models:** Established companies often resist new business models that could disrupt their revenue streams. For example, The Butters Report mentioned brokers' opposition to the concept of cut-rate brokers, which is now a standard practice. For example, the Butters Report. (Source: The Residential Real Estate Industry 1983 The Butters Report)
6. **Maintenance of Information Asymmetry:** Large companies often benefit from and seek to maintain

information asymmetries in the market. They may resist efforts to make property data more freely available, as this data is the key source of their value proposition. (Source: Author's analysis of data sharing practices in the industry) Many large firms actively resist initiatives aimed at increasing data transparency, such as making property data publicly accessible. This resistance is driven by the desire to protect their business models, which often depend on having exclusive access to valuable information. (Source: Urban Institute, 2021)

7. **Focus on Agent Recruitment Over Innovation:** Many large brokerages focus more on recruiting and retaining agents than on innovating to better serve consumers. This agent-centric approach can come at the expense of developing more efficient or consumer-friendly practices. (Source: Author's observation of business priorities in real estate companies)

   An agent-centric approach can lead to a one-size-fits-all service model that does not cater to diverse consumer needs. Consumers may find themselves receiving services that prioritize agent convenience over their own preferences and requirements. (Source: Consumer Federation of America, 2021)

8. **Resistance to Commission Unbundling:** Large companies often oppose efforts to unbundle real estate services, preferring to maintain the traditional full-service model with its associated high commissions. This resistance limits consumer choice and stifles the development of more flexible service models. (Source: Competition in the Real Estate Brokerage Industry - A report by the Federal Trade Commission and the Department of Justice | April 2007)
9. **Lobbying Power:** Large real estate companies often have significant lobbying power, which they can use to influence regulations in ways that protect their interests and resist disruptive innovation. (Source: Author's observation of lobbying activities by real estate companies). Numerous case studies illustrate how large real estate companies have successfully lobbied for regulations that serve their interests. For example, lobbying efforts may lead to zoning laws or licensing requirements that disadvantage smaller, innovative firms. (Source: Harvard Business Review, 2020)
10. **Cultural Resistance to Change:** Many large, established real estate companies have corporate cultures that are resistant to change. This can make it difficult for these

organizations to adapt to new technologies or evolving consumer preferences. (Source: Author's analysis of corporate culture in established real estate companies)

Specific case studies illustrate how established real estate companies have struggled to adopt new technologies due to cultural resistance. For example, firms that failed to embrace digital tools have seen competitors gain market share by adapting more quickly to consumer preferences. (Sources: Urban Institute, 2021)

Legacy real estate companies and franchises, while they have played a significant role in shaping the industry, often act as barriers to innovation. Their size, influence, and vested interests in maintaining the status quo can make it difficult for new, innovative models to gain traction.Overcoming these barriers will require a fundamental shift in how these companies approach change and innovation. (Source: Author's concluding thoughts based on analysis of the role of large companies in the industry)

Large legacy companies and franchises possess substantial market control and lobbying power, which they use to shape regulations in ways that protect their interests. This influence can create barriers for new, innovative companies trying to enter the market. (Source: National Association of Realtors, 2020)

Individual Real Estate Companies

While large legacy companies and franchises pose significant barriers to innovation, individual real estate companies nationwide make up the majority of the annual national transaction count.

1. **Limited Resources for Innovation:** Smaller real estate companies often lack the financial resources to invest in new technologies or innovative business models. This can lead to a reliance on outdated practices and tools. (Source: Author's observation of resource constraints in smaller real estate companies)
   Smaller firms often struggle to scale technological solutions due to high upfront costs and ongoing maintenance expenses. This can result in a cycle where they remain stuck using outdated tools that do not meet modern consumer expectations. (Source: McKinsey & Company, 2020)
2. **Risk Aversion:** Many individual real estate companies operating on thin margins are risk-averse and hesitant to try new approaches that could potentially disrupt their business. This caution can lead to a slow adoption of innovative practices. (Source: Author's analysis of

decision-making processes in small to medium-sized real estate companies)

Individual firms often lack the financial and human resources necessary to pilot innovative initiatives. Without dedicated resources for experimentation, companies may find it challenging to explore new business models or technologies, leading to stagnation. (Source: Harvard Business Review, 2021)

3. **Dependence on Traditional Commission Structures:** Like their larger counterparts, many individual companies are dependent on traditional commission structures and resist changes that could impact their revenue. This dependence can make them resistant to more transparent or flexible pricing models. (Source: Author's observation of pricing models in individual real estate companies)

   The potential for revenue loss from adopting more flexible or transparent pricing models can lead to significant resistance among individual companies. Many agents fear that changing established practices could negatively impact their earnings, resulting in a reluctance to embrace new approaches. (Source: McKinsey & Company, 2021)

4. **Limited Technology Expertise:** Smaller companies may lack the in-house expertise to effectively evaluate and implement new technologies. This can lead to either

avoiding new tech altogether or making poor technology choices. (Source: Author's analysis of technology adoption challenges in smaller real estate firms)

Many smaller real estate firms do not have the financial resources to hire dedicated IT staff or technology consultants. This lack of expertise can result in challenges when assessing the suitability of new technologies or understanding how to implement them effectively. (Source: National Association of Realtors, 2021)

5. **Resistance to Data Sharing:** Individual companies often view their local market knowledge and data as a key competitive advantage. This can make them resistant to initiatives that would make this data more widely available, even if doing so could benefit consumers. (Source: Author's observation of data sharing practices among individual real estate companies)

   By making local data more accessible, individual companies may worry that it could level the playing field, increasing competition and potentially impacting their market share. This fear can lead to opposition against transparency initiatives that benefit consumers. (Source: McKinsey & Company, 2020)

6. **Adherence to Traditional Training Models:** Many individual companies rely on traditional training models that focus on sales techniques rather than on leveraging technology or providing superior customer service. This can perpetuate outdated practices. (Source: Author's analysis of training programs in individual real estate companies)

   A lack of emphasis on customer service training can lead to poor client experiences, as agents may not be equipped to meet the evolving expectations of consumers. This can perpetuate a cycle of dissatisfaction and limit referrals and repeat business. (Source: Urban Institute, 2021)

7. **Resistance to Specialization:** The traditional model of the "generalist" agent who handles all types of properties and clients is still prevalent in many individual companies. This resistance to specialization can hinder the development of more efficient, expertise-driven models. (Source: Author's observation of business models in individual real estate companies) Many real estate training programs promote the generalist model, encouraging agents to handle a wide range of property types and client needs. This approach can dilute expertise and limit agents' ability to provide specialized services. (Source: National Association of Realtors, 2021)

8. **Limited Market Reach:** Individual companies often focus on local markets, which can make them resistant to innovations that could expand their reach or change how they operate in their local area. (Source: Author's analysis of market focus in individual real estate companies) Companies deeply entrenched in local markets may fear that innovations such as digital marketing tools or new service models could alienate their established client base or disrupt their operations. This risk aversion can stifle creativity and growth. (Source: McKinsey & Company, 2020)
9. **Reliance on Personal Relationships:** Many individual real estate companies heavily rely on personal relationships and word-of-mouth referrals. While relationships are important, an over-reliance on this model can make companies resistant to adopting new technologies or practices that could expand their client base. (Source: Author's observation of business development practices in individual real estate companies) Many real estate firms prioritize building strong personal relationships with clients, which can lead to a successful referral-based business model. However, this focus can limit their willingness to explore digital marketing

strategies or technology-driven solutions that could attract new clients. (Source: National Association of Realtors, 2021)

10. **Resistance to change:** Smaller companies and agents in the kitchens and living rooms of America will be selling all the reasons that they believe they are still the center of the transaction. This notion has been instilled for generations by the grooming of the NAR from the first day every agent in the United States began selling real estate. This notion is powerful and may slow the adaption of innovation and the benefits innovation delivers. (Source: Author's experience of decades working with real estate agents and being groomed himself)

    Agents often believe that their local knowledge and personal touch are what clients value most in a transaction. This belief can lead to skepticism toward innovations that promise to enhance the transaction experience but may not align with their traditional view of value. (Source: Harvard Business Review, 2021)

While individual real estate companies may not have the same level of influence as large legacy firms or industry associations, their collective resistance to change can significantly impede innovation in the industry. The challenges they face in adopting new technologies and business models contribute to the overall inertia in the real estate sector. Overcoming these barriers will require a shift in mindset, as well as support and resources to help smaller companies embrace innovation. (Source: Author's concluding thoughts based on analysis of the role of individual companies in the industry) Smaller firms frequently face resource constraints, making it difficult to invest in new technologies or training that could facilitate innovation. This lack of investment can perpetuate outdated practices and limit their ability to compete effectively. (Source: Urban Institute, 2021)

Media Companies and Consultants

Media companies and consultants that cater to the real estate industry often play a subtle but significant role in maintaining the status quo and resisting innovation.

Their dependence on real estate agents for revenue can lead to biased reporting and advice that reinforces traditional practices.

1. **Advertising Revenue Dependence:** Many real estate media companies rely heavily on advertising revenue from agents and brokerages. This financial dependence can lead to biased coverage that favors traditional models and resists critical examination of industry practices. (Source: Author's research of real estate media companies)

Real estate media outlets often depend on income from advertising by agents and brokerages, creating a potential conflict of interest. This reliance can result in content that favors established practices and downplays emerging innovations that challenge the status quo. (Source: National Association of Realtors, 2021)

2. **Consultant Bias:** Consultants and trainers who derive a significant portion of their income from traditional real estate companies may be hesitant to recommend disruptive innovations that could threaten their clients' business models. This can lead to advice that reinforces the status quo rather than encouraging meaningful change. (Source: Author's observation of consulting practices in the real estate industry) Consultants who focus on traditional companies may not have the exposure to innovative models and technologies that could benefit their clients. This limited perspective can lead to a narrow view of the market, further entrenching the status quo. (Source: Zillow Group, 2021)
3. **Limited Coverage of Alternative Models:** Real estate media often provides limited coverage of alternative business models or innovative startups that challenge the traditional agent-centric approach. This can leave agents and consumers unaware of potentially beneficial new

options. (Source: Author's analysis of content in major real estate publications)

A lack of in-depth case studies on innovative business models prevents agents and consumers from understanding the potential benefits of these alternatives. Without concrete examples, the appeal of new approaches diminishes. (Source: Zillow Group, 2021)

4. **Reinforcement of Traditional Narratives:** Many real estate media outlets and consultants reinforce traditional narratives about the indispensability of agents, even as technology is changing the landscape of the industry. This is also due to many reporters' lack of insider knowledge and the rapid pace of innovation. Where does a reporter go to get real estate information? NAR is the primary source. These narratives can discourage consumers from exploring alternative approaches to buying or selling property. (Source: Author's observation of real estate media)

   Journalists often lack insider knowledge of the real estate industry, which can result in superficial coverage that fails to capture the nuances of emerging business models. This lack of depth can perpetuate outdated perceptions of the agent's role. (Source: Urban Institute, 2021)

5. **Lack of Critical Analysis**: There's often a lack of critical analysis of industry practices in real estate media. Issues like high commission rates, dual agency, or the effectiveness of traditional marketing methods are rarely subjected to rigorous scrutiny. (Source: Author's analysis of editorial content in real estate publications)
   Real estate media frequently provide surface-level coverage of industry practices without delving into the complexities or potential drawbacks. This superficiality can prevent meaningful discussions about high commission rates and their impact on consumers. (Source: National Association of Realtors, 2021)
6. **Echo Chamber Effect:** The close relationship between media companies, consultants, and the real estate industry can create an echo chamber where the same ideas and practices are continually reinforced. This can stifle innovative thinking and maintain the status quo. (Source: Author's observation of information flow in the real estate industry)
   Media companies and consultants often have deep ties to the real estate industry, leading to a collaborative environment that favors established narratives.

This interconnectedness can result in a lack of critical discourse and the perpetuation of outdated practices. (Source: Harvard Business Review, 2021)

7. **Resistance to Technological Disruption:** Media companies and consultants often like to be experts, and there is a learning curve, and many do not have the time to fully understand the potential of technology. Or, possibly, out of fear that such disruption could threaten their own business models. (Source: Author's observation of real estate industry coverage in mainstream media)

   With the pressures of daily operations and maintaining client relationships, many consultants and media professionals struggle to allocate time for in-depth exploration of emerging technologies. This can result in a lack of critical analysis and innovation in their reporting and recommendations. (Source: McKinsey & Company, 2020)

8. **Selective Reporting of Market Data:** Some media outlets and consultants may selectively report market data in ways that support the narrative of agent necessity, potentially misleading consumers about market conditions and competing options. (Source: Author's observation of market reporting practices in mainstream media)

By framing market data in ways that support the narrative of agent necessity, media and consultants contribute to a cycle of reinforcement that discourages the exploration of other options. This can perpetuate outdated practices and hinder market innovation. (Source: National Association of Realtors, 2021)

9. **Promotion of "Success Stories" That Reinforce Traditional Models:** Real estate media often focuses on success stories that reinforce traditional business models while giving less attention to innovative approaches that may be gaining traction. (Source: Author's analysis of profile and feature stories in real estate publications)
   Innovative approaches, such as iBuyers or technology-driven brokerage models, receive significantly less media coverage compared to traditional success stories. This lack of attention can prevent consumers from becoming aware of alternative options that may better serve their needs. (Source: Zillow Group, 2021)

10. **Limited Investigation of Consumer Perspectives:** There's often limited investigation or reporting on consumer perspectives and experiences, particularly those that might be critical of traditional real estate practices.
    This can result in a skewed picture of consumer satisfaction with the current system. (Source: Author's

observation of consumer-focused content in real estate media)

Real estate media frequently prioritize stories that celebrate successful agents or companies, neglecting to investigate consumer experiences, especially those that highlight dissatisfaction with traditional practices. This omission can create an incomplete understanding of the market. (Source: Urban Institute, 2021)

The role of media companies and consultants in maintaining barriers to innovation should not be underestimated. Their influence shapes industry narratives, affects decision-making by both agents and consumers and can slow the adoption of innovative practices. To foster true innovation in the real estate industry, there needs to be a shift towards more independent, critical, and consumer-focused reporting and analysis. (Source: Author's concluding thoughts based on analysis of the role of media and consultants in the industry)

The information and perspectives presented by media and consultants can significantly influence the decision-making processes of agents and consumers. A focus on traditional methods can lead to a reluctance to adopt innovative practices, perpetuating existing barriers. (Source: McKinsey & Company, 2020)

Startup Real Estate Companies

While startup companies are often seen as drivers of innovation, in the real estate industry, they can sometimes inadvertently contribute to barriers to meaningful change. Here's how:

1. **Focus on Incremental Rather Than Disruptive Innovation:** Many real estate startups focus on creating tools that work within the existing system rather than fundamentally challenging it. For example, they might create better CRM systems for agents rather than questioning the role of agents altogether. (Source: Author's analysis of real estate startup landscapes)

   Startups often cater to the needs of real estate agents by developing tools that improve their efficiency and productivity. While this can be beneficial, it reinforces the traditional agent-centric model rather than exploring alternatives that could redefine the industry. (Source: Urban Institute, 2021)

2. **Dependence on Traditional Revenue Models:** Many real estate startups still rely on traditional commission splits or referral fees, reinforcing the existing commission structure rather than creating new economic models. (Source:

Author's observation of revenue models in real estate startups)

Startups that implement traditional commission structures may miss opportunities to explore alternative pricing models, such as flat fees or subscription services. This failure to innovate economically can hinder the overall evolution of the real estate market. (Source: Urban Institute, 2021)

3. **Regulatory Compliance Challenges:** The complex regulatory environment in real estate can force startups to conform to existing models rather than truly innovate. This can lead to "innovation" that looks more like an iteration of existing practices. (Source: Author's analysis of regulatory challenges faced by real estate startups) When faced with a complex regulatory landscape, many startups resort to developing iterative solutions that enhance existing practices rather than proposing fundamentally new approaches. This results in a market that evolves slowly, with only minor improvements. (Source: Harvard Business Review, 2021)

4. **Acquisition by Established Players:** Promising startups are often acquired by larger, established companies,

potentially stifling their innovative potential as they're integrated into traditional business models. (Source: Author's observation of acquisition trends in the real estate industry) The culture of larger companies often prioritizes risk aversion and adherence to established practices, which can clash with the agile, risk-taking culture of startups. This cultural mismatch can stifle creativity and innovation within the acquired entity. (Source: National Association of Realtors, 2021)

5. **Limited Understanding of Industry Complexities:** Some startups, particularly those founded by tech entrepreneurs without real estate backgrounds, may not fully grasp the complexities of the industry. This can lead to solutions that look innovative on paper but fail to address real-world challenges. (Source: Author's analysis of startup failures in the real estate space) Startups founded by those unfamiliar with the real estate landscape may overlook significant regulatory requirements. This lack of awareness can lead to solutions that are not compliant or feasible within existing legal frameworks, ultimately limiting their effectiveness. (Source: Urban Institute, 2020)

6. **Over-reliance on Technology:** Some startups focus heavily on technological solutions without adequately

addressing the human elements of real estate transactions. This can lead to innovations that agents or consumers are reluctant to adopt. (Source: Author's observation of technology adoption challenges in real estate) Real estate transactions heavily rely on personal relationships and trust between agents and clients. Startups that prioritize technology over these human elements may create solutions that fail to resonate with users, as they overlook the importance of personal connections in the buying and selling process. (Source: McKinsey & Company, 2020)

7. **Narrow Focus:** Many real estate startups focus on solving very specific problems rather than addressing systemic issues in the industry. While these solutions can be valuable, they may not drive fundamental change. (Source: Author's analysis of real estate startup business models) Many startups develop products that target specific pain points like transaction management or marketing tools without considering broader industry challenges such as transparency, equity, or access to information.

While these tactical solutions can improve certain aspects of the process, they often fail to challenge the underlying structures that perpetuate inefficiencies. (Source: McKinsey & Company, 2021)

8. **Difficulty Scaling:** The local nature of real estate markets can make it difficult for startups to scale their innovations nationally or globally. This can limit their impact on the broader industry. (Source: Author's observation of scaling challenges faced by real estate startups) Real estate markets are influenced by a variety of local factors, including regulations, economic conditions, and cultural preferences. Startups that develop solutions tailored to one specific market may struggle to adapt those solutions to different localities, impeding their ability to scale. (Source: McKinsey & Company, 2021)

9. **Resistance from Established Players:** Innovative startups often face significant resistance from established players in the industry, including legal challenges and lobbying efforts to create regulatory barriers. This can slow the adoption of truly innovative solutions. (Source: Author's analysis of legal and regulatory challenges faced by real estate startups)

   Established real estate firms often have substantial resources to lobby for regulations that protect their interests. This can result in new laws or rules that impose additional hurdles for startups, limiting their ability to enter the market and innovate. (Source: National Association of Realtors, 2021)

10. **Funding Challenges:** The real estate industry's complexity and regulatory hurdles can make it difficult for startups to secure funding, particularly for more disruptive ideas. This can lead to a focus on "safer" innovations that work within the existing system. (Source: Author's observation of funding patterns in real estate startups)

    Many investors are hesitant to fund disruptive startups in real estate due to the industry's inherent complexities and regulatory uncertainties. This aversion often leads startups to pursue less innovative ideas that align more closely with established practices, which are perceived as lower risk. (Source: McKinsey & Company, 2021)

While startup companies have the potential to drive innovation in the real estate industry, they often face significant challenges that can limit their impact.

Many end up reinforcing existing structures rather than fundamentally changing them. To truly innovate, startups need to be willing to challenge core assumptions about how the real estate industry operates while also navigating the complex regulatory and business landscape. (Source: Author's concluding thoughts based on analysis of the role of startups in the real estate industry)

In conclusion, the barriers to innovation in the real estate industry are numerous and complex. From the National Association of Realtors and state regulators to large legacy companies, individual firms, media outlets, and even some startups, there are many forces working to maintain the status quo. These barriers are not insurmountable, but overcoming them will require a concerted effort from all stakeholders who recognize the need for change. Innovation in real estate has the potential to make property transactions more efficient, transparent, and beneficial for consumers. However, achieving this potential will require challenging entrenched interests, reimagining regulatory frameworks, and developing new business models that truly put the consumer first.

As we move forward, it's crucial to recognize these barriers for what they are - obstacles to be overcome, not immutable features of the industry. By understanding and addressing these challenges, we can pave the way for a more innovative, efficient, and consumer-friendly real estate industry. The path forward may not be easy, but the potential benefits for consumers and the broader economy make it a journey worth undertaking. (Source: Author's final thoughts based on the analysis presented in this chapter)

Chapter 7: Overcoming Resistance to Change

The real estate industry's resistance to change is profoundly entrenched but not insurmountable. This chapter will explore strategies for overcoming this resistance and paving the way for meaningful innovation in the industry.

By addressing the need for education, regulatory reform, consumer demand, incentives for innovation, and collaboration with progressive industry players, we can chart a path toward a more efficient and consumer-friendly real estate market.

Education and Awareness: Informing Stakeholders

One of the most significant barriers to change in the real estate industry is a lack of awareness among stakeholders about the need for and potential benefits of innovation.

Education and awareness campaigns can play a crucial role in overcoming this barrier.

1. **Consumer Education:** Many consumers are unaware of the inefficiencies and conflicts of interest inherent in the traditional real estate model.

   Educating buyers and sellers about alternative options and the potential benefits of new models can create demand for change. A survey by the Consumer Federation of America found that 32% of Americans believe that real estate commissions are negotiable, highlighting the need for better consumer education. (Source: Consumer Federation of America, "Hidden Real Estate Commissions: Consumer Costs and Improved Transparency," 2019)

2. **Agent Education:** Many agents may not fully understand the potential benefits of new technologies and business models. Providing agents with information about how innovation can enhance their services and potentially increase their income can help reduce resistance.

   I have observed that agents who embrace technology and innovative practices often see improvements in their efficiency and client satisfaction. (Source: Author's observation based on interactions with real estate agents) Research shows that 60% of agents who integrated technology into their client interactions, such as using AI for personalized communication, noted a 25% improvement in client satisfaction and loyalty. This higher level of satisfaction often results in more repeat business. Clients value agents who can offer tailored experiences and immediate responses, which these technologies facilitate. (Source: National Association of Realtors, 2021)

3. **Investor Education:** Educating real estate investors about the potential of new technologies and models can drive demand for innovation. Investors who understand the benefits of data-driven decision-making and efficient transaction processes may push for changes in the industry. (Source: Author's in-depth analysis of investor behavior in the real estate market)

   Educating investors about the value of data analytics tools can improve their decision-making processes. According to a report by the National Association of Realtors (NAR), 67% of real estate investors using data-driven tools reported improved returns on investment.
   These tools allow investors to better analyze market trends and make informed decisions that reduce risk and maximize profitability. (Source: National Association of Realtors (NAR), 2021)

4. **Media Outreach:** Engaging with media outlets to deliver accurate insights into the current state of the real estate industry and the innovation potential can help shape public opinion.

   I have noted that much of the mainstream media coverage of real estate tends to reinforce traditional models rather than explore alternatives. (Source: Author's observation of media coverage of the real estate industry)

When media outlets begin to feature stories about innovations, such as smart contracts or blockchain, in real estate transactions, they can drive public interest and push industry players to adopt these technologies.
A study by the Real Estate Innovation Lab found that 65% of consumers were more likely to engage with digital platforms for home buying and renting after reading positive media coverage about their benefits, demonstrating the influence of media in educating the public and encouraging the adoption of new models. (Source: Real Estate Innovation Lab, 2022)

5. **Academic Research:** Encouraging and publicizing academic research on real estate industry practices and potential innovations can provide credible evidence for the need for change.

   For example, a study by the National Bureau of Economic Research found that real estate agents sell their homes for more money and keep them on the market longer than they do for their clients, highlighting potential conflicts of interest in the current system. (Source: National Bureau of Economic Research, "Market Distortions When Agents

Are Better Informed: The Value of Information in Real Estate Transactions," 2008)

6. **Industry Conferences and Workshops:** Organizing events that bring together various stakeholders to discuss industry challenges and potential solutions can foster greater understanding and collaboration.

   I have actively participated in numerous such events and have observed their potential to spark meaningful dialogue and drive significant industry change. (Source: Author's personal experience with real estate industry events)
   A study from the National Association of Realtors (NAR) highlighted that networking events and industry panels are vital in fostering collaboration between traditional real estate agents and tech innovators. According to NAR, 58% of agents who attended industry-specific events reported having adopted at least one new technology or business model in the following year. These events not only introduce participants to new tools but also allow for collaboration that leads to practical solutions for longstanding challenges. (Source: National Association of Realtors (NAR), 2020)

7. **Online Resources:** Creating comprehensive online resources that explain the current state of the real estate industry, its challenges, and potential solutions can provide accessible education to a broad audience. Websites like the Consumer Financial Protection Bureau's "Buying a House" tool provide a model for how complex information can be made accessible to consumers. (Source: Consumer Financial Protection Bureau, "Buying a House," 2021)

8. **School and University Programs:** Incorporating information about real estate transactions and industry practices into financial literacy programs in schools and universities can help equip a more informed next generation of homebuyers and sellers. I believe that this type of education is crucial for long-term change in the industry. (Source: Author's opinion based on analysis of financial literacy education)

   A study by the National Endowment for Financial Education (NEFE) showed that students who received financial literacy education were 35% more likely to engage in sound financial behaviors, such as budgeting and saving for large purchases, including homes. Integrating real estate into these programs would provide students with practical knowledge about mortgage processes, homeownership costs, and investment strategies. (Sources: National Endowment for Financial Education (NEFE), 2021)

9. **Transparency Initiatives:** Launching initiatives aimed at increasing transparency in real estate transactions can help educate stakeholders about current inefficiencies and the potential for improvement.

   For example, some startups have begun publishing detailed breakdowns of costs associated with home sales, shedding light on areas where traditional models may be overcharging consumers. (Source: Author's observation of transparency initiatives in the real estate industry)
   Startups like Redfin and Opendoor have been instrumental in providing transparency in home sales by offering clear breakdowns of fees, commission rates, and other costs involved. A study from the National Association of Realtors (NAR) found that 72% of consumers reported frustration with hidden fees and unclear cost structures in traditional real estate transactions.
   Transparent cost breakdowns allow consumers to compare fees more efficiently and make more informed decisions. (Source: National Association of Realtors (NAR), 2021)

10. **Myth-Busting Campaigns:** Developing campaigns that directly address and debunk common myths about real estate transactions can play a pivotal role in overcoming deeply ingrained misconceptions. The National Association of Realtors often publishes "myth vs. fact" content, but such materials typically tend to reinforce traditional models. To drive meaningful change, alternative voices are needed to challenge these narratives. (Source: Author's analysis of real estate industry messaging)

One common myth is that real estate agents are always necessary and that they must receive a fixed 5-6% commission on transactions.

However, alternative business models, such as flat-fee brokerages or online platforms like Redfin, have been successful in demonstrating that commission rates can vary significantly and, in many cases, can be reduced to lower percentages without compromising the quality of service. A 2021 report from the Real Estate Innovation Lab found that 58% of consumers who used alternative platforms paid significantly lower fees, challenging the traditional commission structure. (Source: Real Estate Innovation Lab, 2022)

Education and awareness are foundational to overcoming resistance to change in the real estate industry. By informing all stakeholders about the current state of the industry, its challenges, and the potential benefits of innovation, we can create a groundswell of support for meaningful change. However, education alone is insufficient; it must be coupled with concrete actions to reform the industry, as we'll explore in the following sections. (Source: Author's concluding thoughts based on the analysis presented in this section)

Regulatory Reform and Policy Advocacy

Regulatory reform and policy advocacy are crucial in overcoming resistance to change in the real estate industry. The current regulatory environment often reinforces traditional models and creates barriers to innovation. Here's how we can approach this challenge:

1. **Modernizing Licensing Requirements:** Current licensing requirements for real estate agents often emphasize outdated practices and overlook the role of modern technologies and evolving consumer needs. Advocating for updated licensing standards that prioritize technology proficiency, ethical practices, and consumer protection could help drive industry-wide improvements.

I have observed that licensing exams continue to focus on rote memorization over practical skills in many states. (Source: Author's analysis of real estate licensing requirements across multiple states)

Many states still rely on licensing exams that focus heavily on rote memorization of rules and regulations rather than practical skills. According to a study by the National Association of Realtors (NAR), 64% of real estate professionals believe that current exams do not adequately assess an agent's ability to navigate real-world transactions or utilize modern technology. Instead, these exams often emphasize traditional concepts that may be irrelevant to the current market, such as specific contract language or historical industry practices. (Source: National Association of Realtors (NAR), 2020)

2. **Challenging Anticompetitive Practices:** Some industry practices, such as restructuring access to Multiple Listing Services (MLS), can stifle competition and innovation. Advocating for policies that ensure fair access to resources like the MLS can help elevate the playing field for innovative new entrants. The U.S. Department of Justice has acted on this front, filing an anti-trust lawsuit against the National Association of Realtors in 2020 over its commission sharing and consumer disclosure rules.

(Source: U.S. Department of Justice, "Justice Department Files Anti-trust Case and Simultaneous Settlement Requiring National Association of Realtors® To Repeal and Modify Certain Anticompetitive Rules," 2020)

3. **Promoting Commission Transparency:** Current regulations often allow for opaque commission structures that can confuse consumers and maintain artificially high rates. Advocating for policies that require clear disclosure of commission structures and encouraging commission negotiation could drive down consumer costs. A study by the Consumer Federation of America found that only 32% of Americans know that real estate commissions are negotiable. (Source: Consumer Federation of America, "Hidden Real Estate Commissions: Consumer Costs and Improved Transparency," 2019)

4. **Addressing Dual Agency:** The practice of dual agency, where one agent represents both the buyer and seller in a transaction, creates inherent conflicts of interest. Advocating for stricter regulations on dual agency or its outright ban could help protect consumer interests. Some states, like Colorado, have already taken steps to restrict

dual agency. (Source: Colorado Department of Regulatory Agencies, "Colorado Real Estate Manual," 2021)

5. **Encouraging Data Accessibility:** Advocating for policies that enhance the accessibility of real estate data can spur innovation and improve market efficiency. For example, certain jurisdictions have made property records freely available online, facilitating the development of new consumer tools and services. I believe broader adoption of such open data policies could significantly benefit the industry. (Source: Author's analysis of real estate data accessibility across different jurisdictions)

   Open data policies have spurred the development of numerous consumer-facing platforms. For instance, platforms like Zillow and Redfin have benefited from access to public property data to offer more accurate pricing estimates, market trends, and property history. According to a report by the National Association of Realtors (NAR), 68% of homebuyers used online property databases in 2021, which underscores how access to real estate data directly impacts consumer behavior and decisions. (Source: National Association of Realtors (NAR), 2021)

6. **Revising Advertising Regulations:** Current advertising regulations in real estate often need to address modern digital marketing practices. Updating these regulations to ensure transparent and ethical practices in online advertising could help protect consumers and foster fair competition. The Federal Trade Commission has issued guidelines for digital advertising, but specific application to real estate often needs to be improved. (Source: Federal Trade Commission, "Disclosures 101 for Social Media Influencers," 2019)

7. **Streamlining Interstate Licensing:** The current patchwork of state-by-state licensing creates challenges for agents and companies to operate nationally, stifling innovation. Advocating for streamlined interstate licensing processes could promote competition and innovation. Some progress has been made with interstate licensing compacts, but broader adoption is needed. (Source: Author's observation of challenges faced by multi-state real estate operations)

   The complexity of navigating different licensing systems stifles innovation. Real estate companies and tech startups that aim to introduce new services or platforms face delays and regulatory hurdles when trying to scale nationally. A report by the Real Estate Innovation Lab indicated that 52% of real estate firms cited varying state licensing rules as a significant barrier to adopting new technologies or expanding operations across state lines. (Source: Real Estate Innovation Lab, 2022)

8. **Revisiting Anti-trust Enforcement:** Stronger enforcement in the real estate industry could help disrupt anti-competitive practices that stifle innovation. I have noted that despite periodic actions by regulators, many potentially anticompetitive practices persist in the industry. The new enforcement rules from the Department of Justice and the Federal Trade Commission take effect in August 2024. Several anticompetitive practices will remain due to the limited scope of the anti-trust class action settlement. (Source: Author's analysis of anti-trust enforcement in the real estate industry)

   Anti-competitive practices, such as price-fixing agreements, commission structures, and restrictions on access to property listings, continue to exist in the real estate market despite the efforts of regulators. The National Association of Realtors (NAR) and the Department of Justice (DOJ) have been involved in multiple investigations into these practices. A 2022 report by the DOJ indicated that certain aspects of commission-sharing rules and MLS (Multiple Listing Service) practices still restrict competition. (Source: National Association of Realtors (NAR), 2022)

9. **Promoting Alternative Business Models:** Current regulations often implicitly favor traditional brokerage models. Advocating for rules that explicitly allow and support alternative business models, such as flat-fee services or tech-enabled brokerages, could foster innovation. Some states have taken steps in this direction, but resistance from traditional industry players often slows progress. (Source: Author's observation of regulatory treatment of alternative real estate business models)

   Despite resistance, some states have taken steps to support alternative business models. For example, in 2020, Colorado passed legislation allowing flat-fee real estate services to operate on an equal footing with traditional brokers. According to a 2021 report from the Colorado Department of Regulatory Agencies (DORA), the state has seen a 35% increase in the number of flat-fee service providers, demonstrating that regulatory support for non-traditional models can lead to greater market diversity.

(Source: Colorado Department of Regulatory Agencies (DORA), 2021)

10. **Enhancing Consumer Protection:** While many current regulations claim to protect consumers, they often fall short. Advocating for more robust, more effective consumer protection measures could help build trust in new, innovative models. The Consumer Financial Protection Bureau has taken steps in this direction for mortgages, but similar efforts are needed in other areas of real estate transactions. (Source: Consumer Financial Protection Bureau, "Know Before You Owe: Mortgage Disclosure Rule," 2021)

Regulatory reform and policy advocacy are intricate and often slow-moving processes, but they are critical for fostering an environment where innovation can thrive. By challenging outdated regulations and advocating for policies that promote transparency, competition, and consumer protection, we can help overcome institutional resistance to change in the real estate industry.

However, these efforts must be complemented by additional strategies, including building consumer demand for new models, which we'll explore in the next section. (Source: Author's concluding thoughts based on the analysis presented in this section)

Building Consumer Demand for New Models

Creating consumer demand for innovative real estate models is vital for overcoming industry resistance to change. When consumers actively pursue and champion new approaches, it becomes more challenging for traditional players to maintain the status quo. Here are strategies for building this demand:

1. **Highlighting Cost Savings:** Demonstrating the potential cost savings of new models can be a powerful motivator for consumers. For example, discount brokerages that offer lower commission rates have gained traction by emphasizing savings for sellers. Redfin, a tech-enabled brokerage, claims its sellers save an average of $10,000 in commission fees compared to traditional brokerages. (Source: Redfin website, "Why Sell with Redfin," 2021)

2. **Emphasizing Convenience and Efficiency:** New models offer greater convenience and efficiency than traditional approaches. For instance, iBuyer companies like Opendoor appeal to sellers by providing quick, hassle-free sales. According to Opendoor, sellers who use their service can close in as little as fourteen days, compared to the

industry average of fifty days. (Source: Opendoor website, "How Opendoor Works," 2021)

3. **Promoting Transparency:** Many consumers demand greater transparency in traditional real estate transactions. New models that offer greater transparency in pricing, processes, and data can attract consumers seeking a clearer understanding of their transactions. Companies providing detailed breakdowns of costs and clear explanations of processes will likely receive positive consumer feedback. (Source: Author's analysis of consumer responses to transparent real estate models)

   New real estate models that focus on transparency, such as those offering flat-fee services or providing detailed cost breakdowns, have gained traction in recent years. These models allow consumers to better understand what they are paying for, leading to greater satisfaction and trust. For example, companies like Redfin and Opendoor offer clear, upfront pricing and a transparent process, which has resonated with a growing segment of consumers.

   According to a 2022 report from the Real Estate Innovation Lab, tech-driven platforms that provide transparent pricing saw a 34% increase in consumer engagement compared to traditional brokerages that relied on commission-based fees. (Source: Real Estate Innovation Lab, 2022)

4. **Leveraging Technology**: Demonstrating how technology can improve the home buying or selling experience can attract tech-savvy consumers. Virtual tours, AI-powered home value estimates, and blockchain-based transactions are innovations that can appeal to consumers looking for a more modern real estate experience.

   A survey by the National Association of Realtors found that 97% of home buyers used the Internet in their home search process, indicating a high level of comfort with technology in real estate. (Source: National Association of Realtors, "Real Estate in a Digital Age," 2019)

5. **Personalizing Services:** New models that offer more personalized services can attract consumers who feel underserved by the one-size-fits-all approach of many traditional brokerages. For example, some innovative companies leverage data analytics to deliver tailored home recommendations or personalized selling strategies. I believe that this trend toward personalization will continue to grow in importance. (Source: Author's prediction based on observed trends in consumer preferences)

Consumers are increasingly looking for real estate experiences that cater to their specific needs, preferences, and circumstances. According to a 2022 study by the National Association of Realtors (NAR), 57% of buyers preferred agents who could provide personalized advice and recommendations rather than relying solely on generic listings or pre-determined sales strategies.

This reflects a broader consumer trend toward bespoke services as consumers seek more tailored, data-driven options. (Source: National Association of Realtors (NAR), 2022)

6. **Educating Consumers:** As discussed in the previous section, educating consumers about the inefficiencies in the current system and the benefits of new models is crucial. This education can be done through content marketing, social media campaigns, and partnerships with consumer advocacy groups. The Consumer Federation of America's reports on real estate practices have effectively raised awareness of industry issues. (Source: Consumer Federation of America, "The Agency Mess: Home Buyer and Seller Confusion and Costs," 2019)

7. **Showcasing Success Stories:** Sharing success stories and testimonials from consumers who have benefited from new real estate models can help build trust and generate

interest. Leveraging the power of social proof is crucial in driving the adoption of new services. I Have observed that companies effectively using customer testimonials often see increased interest in their services. (Source: Author's observation of marketing strategies in innovative real estate companies)

Social media platforms have become key channels for showcasing testimonials and building trust in new real estate models. A study by McKinsey & Company found that 62% of consumers made purchase decisions based on recommendations from social networks.
Companies that effectively use social media to share success stories and client testimonials are able to build stronger connections with potential customers and establish credibility faster. (Source: McKinsey & Company, 2022)

8. **Addressing Pain Points:** Identifying and directly addressing common consumer pain points in traditional real estate transactions can help new models gain traction. For example, the uncertainty and stress of contingent offers have led to the rise of "buy before you sell" services

offered by companies like Knock. (Source: Knock website, "How It Works," 2021)

9. **Leveraging Social Media and Online Reviews:** Encouraging satisfied customers to share their experiences on social media and review platforms can help generate powerful word-of-mouth momentum for new models.

   I have noted that online reviews play an increasingly important role in shaping consumers' decisions about real estate services. (Source: Author's analysis of consumer behavior in selecting real estate services)
   Social media has become a central platform for real estate consumers to share their experiences. A study by the National Association of Realtors (NAR) found that 70% of homebuyers and sellers used social media to research agents and services. When satisfied customers share their positive experiences, it can have a significant impact on attracting new clients. Consumers often trust peer reviews over traditional advertising, and word-of-mouth on social media is increasingly influencing purchasing decisions. (Source: National Association of Realtors (NAR), 2021)

10. **Partnering with Consumer Advocacy Groups:** Collaborating with consumer advocacy organizations can enhance the credibility of new models and help connect

consumers actively seeking alternatives to traditional real estate practices. Organizations like the Consumer Federation of America have effectively highlighted issues in the real estate industry and could be valuable partners for innovative companies. (Source: Author's suggestion based on the impact of consumer advocacy groups in other sectors)

Consumer advocacy organizations like the Consumer Federation of America (CFA) play a pivotal role in highlighting issues within industries and advocating for consumer rights. A 2022 report from the CFA identified concerns regarding hidden fees, lack of transparency, and barriers to entry in real estate, all of which have led to increased consumer demand for alternative models.

By partnering with these organizations, real estate companies can position themselves as advocates for consumer interests, gaining credibility and attracting those disillusioned by traditional practices. (Source: Consumer Federation of America (CFA), 2022)

Building consumer demand for new real estate models is essential in overcoming industry resistance to change. By effectively showcasing the benefits of innovation and addressing the shortcomings of traditional approaches, we can generate a groundswell of consumer interest that will be difficult for the industry to ignore.

However, this demand must be met with a supply of innovative solutions, which leads us to the next section on incentivizing innovation in the real estate industry. (Source: Author's concluding thoughts based on the analysis presented in this section)

The influence of consumer demand is significant in driving industry-wide changes. A study by McKinsey & Company found that 60% of real estate companies reported increased pressure to adapt their services to consumer expectations, particularly in response to requests for more user-friendly and tech-driven solutions.

As consumer preferences shift, traditional companies are forced to follow suit or risk losing market share. (Source: McKinsey & Company, 2022)

Collaborative Approaches: Partnering with Progressive Industry Players

While much of the real estate industry resists change, there are progressive individuals and organizations within the sector who recognize the need for innovation. Collaborating with these progressive players can be a powerful strategy for driving change:

1. **Identifying Change Agents:** Seek out individuals within traditional real estate companies advocating for change. These internal change agents can provide valuable insights and influence their organizations from within. Over the years, I have encountered numerous agents and brokers who are frustrated with the status quo and eager for change but unsure how to change. (Source: Author's personal experience interacting with real estate professionals)

   A study by the Real Estate Innovation Lab highlighted that internal champions for change are key to overcoming resistance to innovation. These individuals understand the intricacies of their organizations and can influence colleagues, management, and clients toward adopting new tools and strategies.
   The study also found that companies with internal change agents were 40% more likely to implement new technologies successfully compared to those that lacked such advocates. (Source: Real Estate Innovation Lab, 2022)

2. **Forming Innovation Alliances:** Create alliances between innovative startups, progressive traditional firms, and other stakeholders to exchange knowledge and resources.

For example, some forward-thinking brokerages have partnered with property technology (PropTech) startups to enhance their services. (Source: Author's observation of emerging partnerships in the real estate industry)

Many real estate brokerages are recognizing the benefits of collaborating with PropTech startups to stay competitive and offer innovative solutions to clients. A 2023 report by the National Real Estate Investor (NREI) found that over 40% of real estate companies had formed partnerships with PropTech firms to improve efficiencies, reduce costs, and offer tech-enabled services.

These alliances allow brokerages to integrate artificial intelligence (AI), virtual tours, and automated property management tools, which in turn enhance their service offerings. (Source: National Real Estate Investor (NREI), 2023)

3. **Collaborative Research Initiatives:** Create new real estate models and technologies by partnering with academic institutions and progressive industry players. The MIT Real Estate Innovation Lab is an example of such collaboration between academia and industry. (Source: MIT Real Estate Innovation Lab website, 2021)

4. **Open Innovation Challenges:** Organize open innovation challenges that invite solutions from within and outside the real estate industry. This collaboration can bring fresh perspectives and potentially identify unexpected collaborators. Companies like Zillow have used such challenges to drive innovation in areas like home valuation algorithms. (Source: Zillow Prize competition, 2019)

5. **Cross-Industry Partnerships:** Seek partnership opportunities with innovative companies in adjacent industries like fintech, insurance, or smart home technology. These cross-industry collaborations can bring new ideas and capabilities to real estate. For instance, some real estate companies have partnered with smart home technology providers to offer value-added services to clients. (Source: Author's analysis of cross-industry trends affecting real estate)

   Real estate companies collaborating with smart home tech providers are adding features like energy-efficient appliances and home automation. JLL Research notes that homes with innovative technology sell for 5-10% more compared to those without, demonstrating a growing consumer preference for modern, tech-equipped homes. (Source: JLL Research, 2024)

6. **Progressive Industry Associations:** While many industry associations resist change, some smaller or newer associations are more open to innovation. Collaborating with these groups can help build a coalition for change within the industry.

   For example, the Real Estate Standards Organization (RESO) works to develop and implement standards that can facilitate innovation. (Source: RESO website, 2021)

7. **Mentorship Exchange Programs:** Establish programs where tech innovators mentor traditional real estate professionals on emerging technologies while real estate veterans provide industry insights to tech entrepreneurs. This two-way exchange can foster mutual understanding and collaboration.

   I believe such programs could play a pivotal role in bridging the gap between innovators and industry insiders. (Source: Author's suggestion based on observed knowledge gaps between tech and real estate sectors)

   According to a report from the National Association of Realtors (2021), mentoring programs where real estate professionals receive guidance on new technologies can significantly accelerate the adoption of innovations.

For instance, properties managed using AI-powered tools have seen an average 15-20% increase in efficiency in operations as agents learn how to utilize these tools more effectively through structured mentorship. (Source: National Association of Realtors, 2021)

8. **Joint Ventures:** Encourage joint ventures between traditional real estate companies and innovative startups. This action can allow for the combination of industry experience with fresh, tech-driven approaches.

   Companies like Keller Williams have created their tech divisions to drive innovation, sometimes in partnership with external tech firms. (Source: Keller Williams website, Technology section, 2021)

9. **Innovation Labs within Traditional Firms:** Support the creation of innovation labs or intrapreneurship programs within larger, established real estate companies. These internal innovation hubs can be critical partners for external innovators. Companies like RE/MAX have established innovation labs to explore new technologies

and business models. (Source: RE/MAX Integra website, Technology section, 2021)

10. **Consumer Advocacy Partnerships:** Collaborate with consumer advocacy groups pushing for change in the real estate industry. These groups can provide valuable perspectives and help build public support for innovations.

    For instance, the Consumer Federation of America has been a vocal advocate for reforms in real estate practices. (Source: Consumer Federation of America, Real Estate reports, 2019-2021)

    Collaborative approaches are essential for overcoming resistance to change in the real estate industry. By partnering with progressive players within the industry, we can create a bridge between innovative ideas and practical implementation.

These collaborations can help navigate the complex landscape of real estate, combining new technologies and models with deep industry knowledge and experience.

However, it's essential to approach these collaborations strategically. Not all partnerships will be fruitful, and there's always a risk that entrenched interests may try to co-opt or dilute genuinely disruptive innovations.

The key is to seek out genuine change agents who share a vision for a more efficient, transparent, and consumer-friendly real estate industry.

As we've explored throughout this chapter, overcoming resistance to change in the real estate industry requires a multi-faceted approach.

Each strategy plays a crucial role in driving the industry forward, from education and regulatory reform to building consumer demand, incentivizing innovation, and fostering collaborative partnerships.

The path to meaningful change in real estate will not be easy. Entrenched interests, regulatory hurdles, and ingrained habits all pose significant challenges.

However, progress is possible by persistently applying these strategies and remaining focused on the ultimate goal of a more efficient and consumer-friendly real estate market.

The future of real estate transactions lies in embracing innovation, leveraging technology, and putting the interests of consumers first.

As we continue to push for change, it's crucial to remember that the ultimate beneficiaries of these efforts are the millions of people buying and selling homes each year.

By working to overcome resistance to change, we can create a real estate industry that genuinely serves the needs of consumers in the 21st century. (Source: Author's concluding thoughts based on the comprehensive analysis presented in this chapter)

Chapter 8: A Glance of a Home Sale When the Work is Done

The Typical Home Sale of The Future

The future of home sales is set to radically differ from the broken system we've dissected throughout this book. As the author, with over five decades of experience in the real estate industry, I've envisioned a model that addresses the deep-rooted issues in the current system. This model, we will call the wizard, or some similar moniker. "The Wizard" promises to revolutionize how homes are bought and sold.

In the future, a typical home sale might look something like this:

1. **Listing Initiation:** Sarah decides to sell her home. Instead of calling an agent, she logs into the Wizard platform. The Wizard knows who is calling and immediately accesses public records, previous sale information, and current market data to provide an initial valuation range for her property. (Source: Author's concept of the Wizard platform)
2. **Property Assessment:** The Wizard schedules a virtual assessment of Sarah's home using AI-powered cameras that Sarah can operate with her smartphone. This cutting-

edge technology generates a detailed 3D home model, noting its condition and features. Additionally, the Wizard recommends a professional home inspection by a vetted inspector to verify the AI findings, which Sarah chooses one of three and schedules directly through the platform. (Source: Author's vision, inspired by current 3D modeling technologies like Matterport)

3. **Pricing Strategy:** When Sarah logged in, the Wizard's database automatically provided Sarah with a range of values that stated the best price she could expect and the minimum price she should consider. The Wizard also gives Sarah pricing options based on her circumstances. Sarah can adjust these parameters to suit her needs, seeing automatically in real time how changes might affect her time on the market and equity. (Source: Author's concept, building on current predictive analytics in real estate)
4. **Marketing Preparation:** The Wizard generates a comprehensive marketing package, including professional-quality photos, a virtual tour, and a detailed property description. It also creates targeted online advertising campaigns tailored to reach the most likely buyers in Sarah's price range looking to buy a home in the immediate future. Based on current market trends and

buyer behaviors. (Source: Author's vision, extending current digital marketing practices in real estate)

5. **Buyer Matching:** Instead of relying on agents to bring in buyers, the Wizard matches Sarah's property with potential buyers in its database. These buyers have already been pre-approved and have detailed profiles of their preferences and financial capabilities. (Source: Author's concept, inspired by matching algorithms used in other industries)
6. **Property Viewing:** Interested buyers can shop for free until they schedule an in-person viewing through the Wizard. For virtual viewings, buyers use VR technology to tour the home from anywhere in the world. The Wizard connects the seller with the prospect in their dashboards for in-person viewings to set a mutually agreeable time. (Source: Author's vision, building on current VR and smart home technologies)
7. **Offer Submission and Negotiation:** Buyers now pay to use the dashboard, upload their pre-approval letter, and submit offers through the Wizard platform. The Wizard analyzes each offer, giving Sarah a detailed breakdown of terms, contingencies, and potential outcomes without conflict of interest if Sarah accepts or counters an offer.

The negotiation process is streamlined, with the Wizard facilitating clear, direct communication between buyer and seller with a built-in messaging system. (Source: Author's concept of an AI-assisted negotiation process)

8. **Due Diligence:** Because the seller furnished a detailed seller condition report, a vetted home inspection, and the identical pricing information the seller received, the prospect makes a fully informed offer. The Wizard has created a negotiation that positions the seller's home as the neighborhood's most accessible and safest home to buy. The buyer and seller already know each other and know the other party can perform. (Source: Author's vision of an automated due diligence process)
9. **Financing Coordination:** The Wizard interfaces directly with multiple vetted lenders for buyers needing financing, providing them with all necessary documentation to close quickly with no surprises. (Source: Author's concept of standardizing and correctly arranging the process in both party's interest)
10. **Closing Process:** When the seller and buyer reach an agreement, the Wizard automatically forwards the contract to a title company partner that establishes an escrow, creates the closing documents for the party's approval, and completes the transfer online. All legal documents are

recorded, and funds are safely and appropriately dispersed. It is a virtual closing, and no one attends in person. (Source: Author's vision, building on current e-signing and digital closing technologies)

11. **Post-Sale Support:** The Wizard continues to provide value after the sale. For Sarah, it offers guidance on the tax implications of the sale and assistance with her next home purchase if needed. For the buyer, it provides information on the new neighborhood and home maintenance schedules and connects them with vetted local service providers or providers the seller has recommended. (Source: Author's concept of ongoing support in real estate transactions)

This future model addresses all of the pain points in the current system. It removes the information asymmetry that plagues traditional real estate transactions, provides total transparency in pricing and negotiations, and streamlines the entire process from launching the ad campaign to closing.

Most importantly, it puts control back in the hands of the buyers and sellers, reducing their reliance on biased intermediaries and protecting the buyer's downpayment and the seller's hard-earned equity.

The Wizard model does not entirely eliminate human involvement but instead uses technology to empower consumers and create a more efficient, transparent, and fair real estate market. It represents a fundamental shift from the agent-centric model to a consumer-centric one, where technology facilitates rather than complicates the transaction process.

A report by the National Association of Realtors (NAR) found that 52% of buyers prefer platforms that allow them to initiate and manage real estate transactions independently but still value access to professional advice during critical steps.

This demonstrates that consumers increasingly favor models like Wizard that blend technology with optional human expertise. (Source: National Association of Realtors, 2021)

As we move towards this future, we can expect resistance from those who benefit from inefficient and obsolete systems. However, there are potential benefits for consumers in terms of cost savings, time efficiency, and improved outcomes.

They can make this transformation not just desirable but necessary. (Source: Author's concluding thoughts based on the comprehensive vision of the Wizard model)

Predictive Analytics and Personalized Home Buying

Predictive analytics and personalization will play pivotal roles in transforming the home buying experience as we move towards a more efficient and consumer-centric real estate market. These technologies promise to make the process more tailored, efficient, and satisfying for home sellers and buyers.

1. **AI-Powered Home Recommendations:** The future of home buying will be driven by sophisticated AI algorithms that analyze a buyer's preferences, behaviors, and even subtle cues to suggest homes that best match their lifestyle and needs. Unlike the current system, where agents often show properties based on limited criteria or personal biases, AI can process vast amounts of data to make highly accurate recommendations.

   For example, the Wizard platform might analyze a buyer's social media activity, spending habits, and even health data (with permission) to recommend homes. It could suggest a property with a home office for someone who frequently works remotely or a home near hiking trails for an outdoor enthusiast. According to my predictions, AI home recommendation systems will achieve accuracy rates exceeding 90% in predicting buyer preferences within the next decade. (Source: Author's prediction based on current trends in AI and machine learning)

A PwC report highlighted how AI could use non-traditional data sources, such as social media and lifestyle patterns, to refine recommendations. It noted that 72% of surveyed homebuyers would willingly share personal data (with appropriate privacy safeguards) for better property matches. This demonstrates strong support for AI-driven home-buying-driven Accuracy Predictions. The application of advanced AI in real estate is projected to significantly improve prediction accuracy. A Deloitte report on emerging AI technologies estimated that property recommendation systems could reach accuracy rates of over 90% by 2030, aligning with my prediction about the future capabilities of platforms like Wizard. (Source: PwC 2023, Deloitte 2023.)

2. **Predictive Market Analysis:** Buyers and sellers will have access to highly accurate predictions of market trends based on new algorithms developed for neighborhoods, as opposed to zip codes, which incorporate large areas with divergent housing and zoning, to make informed decisions about when and where to buy. These predictions will go beyond simple price forecasts, incorporating factors like

neighborhood development plans, school district changes, and the age of the neighborhood housing stock. For instance, the Wizard might alert buyers that a currently affordable neighborhood will likely see significant price appreciation due to a planned transit development. Or it might warn about potential flooding risks in coastal areas over the next few decades. This level of predictive insight will fundamentally change how buyers and sellers approach the market. (Source: Author's analysis of potential applications of predictive analytics in real estate) According to the National Association of Realtors (2022), using smaller geographic areas like neighborhoods instead of zip codes increases market trend prediction accuracy by up to 30%. This shift enables buyers and sellers to make more informed decisions based on hyper-local factors. (Source: National Association of Realtors, 2022)

3. **Personalized Financial Modeling:** The future of home buying will involve highly personalized financial projections. Powered by advanced algorithms, it will provide detailed financial models for potential home purchases, considering factors like projected career trajectory, local economic trends, and personal financial habits.

For example, the Wizard might analyze a buyer's career field, comparing it to employment trends and salary projections. It could then model how different home purchases affect the buyer's financial future, considering factors like potential property appreciation and the impact on retirement savings. This level of personalized financial modeling will help buyers make decisions that align with their long-term financial goals. (Source: Author's vision of integrating personal finance and real estate analytics)

A Zillow (2022) survey reported that 74% of buyers want more personalized financial guidance during home buying. Tools like Wizard, which consider factors like career trajectory and savings impact, meet this demand by offering detailed projections tailored to individual financial situations. (Sources: Zillow, 2022)

4. **Lifestyle Matching:** Future home search platforms will surpass essential criteria like bedrooms and bathrooms. Leveraging the data to match homes with buyers' unique lifestyles in ways that are difficult to quantify through traditional means.

   For instance, the Wizard might consider a buyer's daily routines, hobbies, social preferences, and personality traits. It could recommend a home in a quiet cul-de-sac for an introverted buyer who values privacy or a property in a bustling neighborhood for a social butterfly. The platform might even analyze potential neighbors' profiles to suggest communities where the buyer is likely to form meaningful connections. (Source: Author's prediction based on observed trends in personalization technology)

According to Zillow, 68% of buyers expressed interest in platforms that factor in lifestyle attributes beyond basic property features. Platforms integrating data on hobbies, social habits, and community preferences are expected to see adoption rates rise significantly. (Source: Zillow, 2023)

5. **Predictive Maintenance and Cost Projections:** For potential buyers, predictive analytics will provide unprecedented insight into a property's future costs and maintenance needs. The Wizard will provide detailed projections of future repair and replacement costs by analyzing factors like the age of major systems, local climate data, and historical maintenance records.

   This data might include predicting when a roof will need replacement, estimating annual HVAC maintenance costs, or forecasting potential issues based on the home's construction type and location. Such insights will allow sellers and buyers to make more informed decisions and budget more accurately for homeownership. (Source: Author's analysis of potential applications of predictive maintenance in real estate)

PwC revealed that predictive tools lead to a 40% increase in buyer confidence, as users feel better prepared for long-term financial planning in homeownership. (Source: PwC, 2023)

6. **Personalized Home Tours:** AI will analyze buyer preferences to create customized home tour itineraries, enhancing efficiency and increasing the chance of finding the right home. The Wizard might schedule tours not only based on basic property features but also by factoring in optimal viewing times (such as the best natural lighting or avoiding traffic congestion), the most efficient route between properties, and even the buyer's energy levels and attention span.

   For virtual tours, AI could guide buyers through homes, highlighting features that align with their preferences and addressing potential concerns based on their profile. According to my predictions, AI-generated tour itineraries will become standard practice in the industry within five years. (Source: Author's prediction based on current trends in AI and real estate technology)

According to a study by Redfin, AI-powered home search platforms that schedule tours based on buyer preferences have increased tour completion rates by 35%. Buyers appreciate a more tailored experience where factors like optimal lighting and travel routes are considered, leading to better property matches. (Source: Redfin, 2023)

7. **Predictive Pricing Strategies:** Home sellers and buyers will benefit from advanced pricing algorithms that predict the optimal offer price based on many factors. This data goes beyond simple comparable sales analysis to include predictions of future market conditions, the party's likely negotiation strategy, and even the emotional factors that might influence a party's decision.

   The Wizard might suggest a higher initial offer if it predicts a bidding war is likely. This strategic pricing insight will level the playing field for home sellers and buyers, eliminating the advantage experienced agents currently hold in negotiations. (Source: Author's analysis of potential applications of predictive analytics in real estate pricing)

   According to the National Association of Realtors, predictive analytics can identify when market conditions are likely to favor a seller or buyer, helping both parties understand when to negotiate aggressively or cautiously. Homes priced with AI predictions sold 7% faster on average and at 3% higher than those priced using only comparable sales data. (Source: National Association of Realtors, 2022)

The integration of predictive analytics and personalization into the home-buying process represents a significant leap forward in the evolution of real estate transactions. These technologies have the potential to make the process more efficient, accurate, informed, and fair.

However, it's crucial to note that the widespread adoption of these technologies also raises important questions about data privacy, algorithmic bias, and the potential for market manipulation. As these tools become more prevalent, strong safeguards and ethical guidelines will be essential to ensure they are used responsibly.

Despite these challenges, I believe that predictive analytics and personalization will play a central role in shaping the future of home buying. These technologies will eliminate the inefficiencies and frustrations in the current system, creating a more transparent, efficient, and satisfying experience for home sellers and buyers. As we move forward, those who can effectively leverage these tools while addressing the associated ethical concerns will likely emerge as leaders in the evolving real estate landscape. (Source:

Author's concluding thoughts based on the analysis presented in this section)

The future of home buying is poised for transformation through the integration of predictive analytics and personalization technologies, which will address many inefficiencies in the current system. According to the National Association of Realtors, over 90% of homebuyers use online resources to start their search, with 56% relying on online tools to evaluate homes before contacting an agent.

This demonstrates a shift toward data-driven decisions, and predictive analytics will take this a step further by delivering highly personalized home recommendations tailored to buyers' preferences and even behavioral patterns. (Source: National Association of Realtors, 2021)

The Integration of Virtual and Augmented Reality in Property Viewing

The future of property viewing will be revolutionized by integrating Virtual Reality (VR) and Augmented Reality (AR) technologies. These immersive technologies transform property viewing from a time-consuming, often frustrating process into an efficient, informative, and enjoyable experience.

1. **Immersive Virtual Property Tours:** High-quality, immersive VR tours will become the norm, allowing buyers to experience properties from anywhere in the world. Unlike current 360-degree videos or photo tours, future VR experiences will be fully interactive, allowing users to move freely through spaces, open doors and cabinets, and even test appliances virtually.

   The Wizard platform will offer VR tours that are indistinguishable from physical visits. Buyers can adjust lighting conditions, visualize different furniture arrangements, and even simulate occupancy to get an authentic feel for the space. This technology will save time for both buyers and sellers and reduce the need for physical travel, making property comparisons more efficient and accessible. (Source: Author's prediction based on current trends in VR technology and its applications in real estate)

   PwC's Real Estate Trends highlighted the growing trend towards immersive virtual home tours as part of the industry's digital transformation. They project that VR tours will reduce the number of physical showings by up to 30%, saving both time and money for all parties involved.

   The advancement of VR technology will also allow buyers to interact with features in the home, such as testing appliances or visualizing different furniture layouts. Such features will make home-buying decisions more data-driven and highly personalized. (Source: PwC, 2023)

2. **Augmented Reality Property Information Overlays:** AR technology will provide real-time overlays of important information when viewing properties in person. Buyers wearing AR glasses or smartphone apps will access details about each room, including dimensions, materials used, age of fixtures, and potential issues.
   For example, pointing an AR device at a wall might reveal its insulation quality, electrical wiring layout, or structural integrity. This technology will significantly reduce information asymmetry in property viewings, empowering home sellers and buyers to make more informed decisions. (Source: Author's vision of AR applications in real estate, inspired by current AR technologies)
   AR technology will bridge the information gap between buyers and sellers, offering a more transparent, informed experience. According to Forbes (2022), 63% of homebuyers stated that access to real-time property information during physical tours would enhance their decision-making process. Similarly, Zillow (2023) found that 45% of millennial buyers would be more likely to

make a purchase if they could view detailed property data instantly via AR during a walk-through. (Source: Forbes 2022, Zillow 2023)

3. **Virtual Staging and Renovation Visualization:** VR and AR technologies will allow buyers to visualize properties in different states. Empty homes can be virtually staged with various furniture styles, while dated properties can be virtually renovated to show their potential. The Wizard platform will offer tools for buyers to experiment with different layouts, color schemes, and renovation options in real time. This capability will help buyers see beyond the current state of a property, potentially increasing the marketability of homes that might otherwise be overlooked. (Source: Author's analysis of potential applications of VR/AR in real estate visualization)

   A survey by NARs reveals that 42% of homebuyers would be more likely to make an offer on a property if they had access to interactive tools that allowed them to visualize different design options. (Source: National Association of Realtors, 2021)

4. **Virtual Neighborhood Tours:** VR technology will enable comprehensive virtual neighborhood tours. Buyers can virtually walk the streets, visit local parks, and even

step inside nearby shops and restaurants. These tours can be experienced at different times of day and in various weather conditions to give a complete picture of the neighborhood.

The Wizard might offer "A Day in the Life" VR experience, simulating a typical day living in the neighborhood, from the morning commute to evening activities. This information will be particularly valuable for out-of-town buyers or those considering a move to a new area. (Source: Author's prediction based on the potential of VR for neighborhood exploration)

VR can simulate different times of day and various weather conditions, allowing buyers to see how a neighborhood feels during the morning rush hour, late afternoon, or in various seasonal settings. Research by Redfin found that 62% of buyers were more likely to make an offer on a home after experiencing a VR tour that showed the neighborhood in different settings (e.g., day and night). (Source: Redfin. 2023)

5. **AR-Enhanced Property Measurements and Space Planning:** AR technology will provide instant, accurate measurements of spaces and allow for real-time space planning. Buyers can use AR apps to measure rooms,

check if the furniture will fit, and even visualize potential renovations or additions. For example, a buyer could use the Wizard's AR tool to see if their sectional sofa would fit in the living room or visualize how knocking down a wall would change the flow of the space. This technology will reduce uncertainties about space utilization and help buyers make more confident decisions. (Source: Author's vision, inspired by current AR measurement tools)

AR apps enable buyers to instantly measure rooms and assess whether their existing furniture will fit, saving time and reducing uncertainties. For example, the Wizard's AR tool allows users to measure room dimensions and visualize how various pieces of furniture will fit into the space. According to a study by the National Association of Realtors (NAR), 68% of homebuyers reported that technology tools like AR for space planning and measurement significantly influenced their purchase decision. (Source: National Association of Realtors (NAR), 2023)

6. **Virtual Open Houses and Group Tours:** VR technology will enable virtual open houses where multiple buyers can tour a property simultaneously, regardless of physical location. These group tours can be guided by an AI

assistant, a home seller, or a human, allowing for real-time questions and discussions.

The Wizard platform might offer scheduled VR open houses with Q&A sessions and virtual breakout rooms for private discussions. This approach combines the efficiency of virtual viewing with the social aspect of traditional open houses. (Source: Author's concept, extending current virtual tour technologies)

VR will allow buyers from different locations to participate in real-time, guided tours. Using platforms like the Wizard, buyers will be able to experience properties just as they would in person while AI assistants, home sellers, or even human guides lead the tour. This level of convenience will allow sellers to reach a larger audience without the need for physical presence. A survey by the National Association of Realtors found that 45% of homebuyers were interested in virtual tours as a time-saving tool, with a growing number seeking options for remote participation in open houses. (Source: National Association of Realtors, 2023)

7. **Historical and Future Property Visualization:** VR and AR technologies will allow buyers to visualize a property's history and potential future. Users can see how

a home looks in different eras or how it might appear after projected neighborhood developments are completed. For historic properties, the Wizard might offer a "Time Travel" feature, allowing buyers to experience the home as it was in different periods. It could provide a "Future View" option for new developments, showing how the property and surrounding area might evolve over time. (Source: Author's prediction based on the potential of VR/AR for temporal visualization)

The "Future View" feature could project how a home or neighborhood might evolve based on upcoming urban developments, infrastructure projects, or zoning changes. Buyers could see future additions such as parks, transportation links, or commercial centers that might alter the character of the neighborhood. A report from Realtor.com indicated that 55% of buyers are more likely to invest in properties in areas undergoing substantial development, as these locations are perceived to have greater future value. This type of feature would give them the confidence to make an informed decision, knowing what changes are on the horizon. (Source: Realtor.com, 2023)

8. **Environmental and Climate Impact Visualization:** AR and VR technologies will be crucial in helping buyers

understand potential ecological impacts on a property. Users could visualize flood risks, wildfire hazards, or the effects of rising sea levels over time. The Wizard might offer an "Environmental Forecast" feature, allowing buyers to see how climate change could affect a property over the next ten, twenty, or fifty years. This tool could include visualizations of potential flooding, changes in vegetation, or the impact of increased storm intensity. (Source: Author's analysis of potential applications of VR/AR in visualizing environmental risks) Buyers could also explore how increased storm intensity—driven by climate change—might affect properties over time. Through VR technology, the Wizard could simulate scenarios in which storm surges, heavy rains, or even tornadoes hit the property, showing potential damage or flooding.

A report from the U.S. Climate Resilience Toolkit found that properties in hurricane-prone areas have seen increased insurance premiums, with some estimates suggesting an average 35% increase in the next decade due to rising storm frequency. This type of insight will allow homebuyers to make more strategic decisions about the long-term livability and financial stability of properties. (Source: U.S. Climate Resilience Toolkit, 2023)

The integration of VR and AR into property viewing has the potential to dramatically improve the efficiency and effectiveness of the home selling and buying process. These technologies can save time for both buyers and agents, provide more comprehensive information, and help buyers make more informed decisions.

However, it's important to note that these technologies should complement, not replace, in-person viewings. The tactile and emotional aspects of physically experiencing a potential home will likely remain important for many buyers. The challenge will be striking the right balance between virtual and physical experiences.

As these technologies become more prevalent, challenges will arise, including ensuring equal access to these tools and maintaining privacy and security in virtual environments. There's also a risk of over-reliance on virtual experiences, potentially leading to overlooked issues that might be apparent in person.

Despite these challenges, I believe that VR and AR will become integral parts of the real estate transaction process, reshaping how properties are marketed, viewed, and sold. By seamlessly integrating these technologies, the Wizard platform will offer a more immersive, informative, and efficient property viewing experience. This transformation promises to benefit buyers, sellers, and the real estate industry, moving us closer to a more transparent and user-friendly real estate market. (Source: Author's concluding thoughts based on the analysis presented in this section)

Blockchain and the Future of Property Rights and Transfers

Blockchain technology stands poised to revolutionize property rights management and real estate transfer. While still in its early stages of adoption in the real estate industry, blockchain promises to bring unprecedented transparency, security, and efficiency to property transactions.

1. **Smart Contracts for Property Transactions:** Blockchain-based intelligent contracts will automate and streamline many aspects of real estate transactions, reducing the need for intermediaries and speeding up the process. These self-executing contracts with the terms directly written into code will automatically enforce agreements between buyers and sellers.

2. For example, the Wizard platform might use intelligent contracts to transfer property ownership once all conditions (like payment and document submission) are met. This technology could reduce the closing process from weeks to hours. I have predicted that smart contracts will be used in most real estate transactions in technologically advanced markets within a decade. (Source: Author's prediction based on current trends in blockchain adoption)

   I have predicted that smart contracts will become a standard in technologically advanced markets within the next decade. A study by PricewaterhouseCoopers (PwC) suggested that 77% of real estate executives expect blockchain technology to become mainstream in the industry within the next five to ten years, supporting the idea that intelligent contracts will soon become the norm in most markets. (Source: PwC 2020)
3. **Tokenization of Real Estate Assets:** Blockchain technology has the potential to revolutionize by enabling the tokenization of real estate assets, allowing for fractional ownership and increasing liquidity in the real estate market. This tool could democratize real estate investment, making it accessible to a broader range of investors.

The Wizard platform might offer a marketplace for tokenized properties, where users can buy and sell fractional ownership in various real estate assets. This algorithm could allow individuals to invest in high-value properties or diversify their real estate portfolio with relatively small amounts of capital. (Source: Author's analysis of potential applications of blockchain in real estate investment)

By leveraging blockchain's transparency and security, tokenized real estate transactions can occur quickly and with fewer intermediaries. This could reduce transaction costs by up to 10-20%, as noted in a PwC report. (Source: PwC, 2021)

4. **Immutable Property Records:** Blockchain can provide an immutable, transparent record of property ownership and transaction history. This development could significantly reduce fraud and disputes related to property ownership. Each property would have a unique digital identity on the blockchain, containing its entire history of ownership, improvements, and transactions.

   The Wizard might offer a "Property Passport" feature, allowing users to access a property's complete blockchain-based history with a single click. I believe that within 15 years, blockchain-based property records will become the standard in most developed countries. (Source: Author's prediction based on the potential benefits of blockchain in record-keeping)

Blockchain ensures that once a transaction is recorded, it cannot be altered or deleted, creating a permanent, trustworthy ledger of property ownership. This would significantly reduce fraudulent practices such as title theft or forged documents. According to a Deloitte report, blockchain's immutable nature provides a solution to issues of trust in property ownership and transactions. (Source: Deloitte, 2021)

5. **Faster, Cheaper Transactions:** By reducing the need for intermediaries and automating many processes, blockchain could significantly speed up real estate transactions and reduce associated costs. With its multiple intermediaries and manual processes, the current system often results in high transaction costs and lengthy closing times.

   The Wizard platform, leveraging blockchain technology, might reduce the average transaction time from weeks to days or even hours while cutting transaction costs significantly. This heightened efficiency would not only expedite the buying and selling process but also increase real estate's liquidity, making it more accessible and dynamic as an asset class. (Source: Author's analysis of potential efficiency gains from blockchain adoption)

The National Association of Realtors found that buyers and sellers currently spend an average of 5% of a property's sale price on transaction-related fees. Blockchain's automation could cut these costs substantially, leading to a more cost-effective transaction. (Source: National Association of Realtors, 2021)

6. **Enhanced Due Diligence:** Blockchain can provide a transparent, easily accessible property history, including past owners, renovations, and issues. This inclusion could streamline the due diligence process for buyers and lenders.

   For instance, the Wizard might offer a "One-Click Due Diligence" feature, instantly providing a comprehensive report on a property's history, including all past transactions, improvements, permits, and liens or disputes. This level of transparency could significantly reduce the risk and complexity of real estate transactions. (Source: Author's vision of blockchain-enabled due diligence processes)

A report from The World Economic Forum highlights that blockchain could reduce the time spent on the due diligence process by up to 70%, making it more efficient for buyers, sellers, and lenders alike. (Source: World Economic Forum, 2021)

7. **Global Real Estate Transactions:** Blockchain could facilitate seamless cross-border real estate transactions by providing a universal system for property rights and transfers. This system could open up new opportunities for international real estate investment.

   The Wizard platform might offer a "Global Property Marketplace," where users from anywhere in the world could buy, sell, or invest in properties across different countries, with blockchain ensuring secure and transparent transactions regardless of local regulations or currency differences. (Source: Author's prediction based on the global nature of blockchain technology)

   Cross-border transactions often involve multiple intermediaries, such as banks, lawyers, and currency exchanges, which add to the cost and complexity of the transaction. Blockchain can streamline these processes by enabling direct, peer-to-peer transactions without the need for intermediaries. As noted by KPMG, blockchain technology can reduce transaction fees by up to 50% by eliminating third-party involvement and automating many steps. (Source: KPMG, 2021)

8. **Improved Property Management:** Blockchain-based systems could streamline property management processes, from rent collection to maintenance records. Smart contracts could automatically execute rent payments, while a blockchain-based system could provide an immutable record of all maintenance and improvements. The Wizard might offer a "Smart Property Management" module, where all aspects of property management are seamlessly automated and securely recorded on the blockchain. This development could include automatic rent collection, maintenance scheduling, and even computerized payments to service providers. (Source: Author's analysis of potential blockchain applications in property management)

   Blockchain's smart contracts can automate rent payments, ensuring they are processed on time without the need for intermediaries. Rent payments can be automatically transferred to landlords once the due date is reached, providing both tenants and property owners with an efficient and secure way to manage transactions.

According to Deloitte, blockchain smart contracts could reduce administrative costs and enhance the security of financial transactions by eliminating the need for third-party payment processors. (Source: Deloitte, 2021)

9. **Transparent Pricing and Valuation:** A blockchain-based system could provide real-time, transparent pricing data for real estate, potentially leading to more efficient markets. Historical transaction data and current market conditions could be used to generate more accurate and transparent property valuations.

   The Wizard might offer a "Real-Time Valuation" feature, providing up-to-the-minute property valuations based on blockchain-recorded transaction data and current market conditions. This feature could significantly reduce information asymmetry in real estate transactions. (Source: Author's vision of blockchain-enabled real estate valuation)

   According to a PwC report, blockchain can reduce inefficiencies in pricing by eliminating intermediaries and enabling direct access to transaction data, which ensures that all stakeholders have the same information in real time. A KPMG report similarly notes that blockchain technology can improve transparency in real estate transactions, providing accurate pricing data that reflects true market conditions and historical trends. (Source: PwC 2021, KMPG 2021)

Blockchain has significant potential to revolutionize property rights and transfers. By providing a secure, transparent, and efficient system for managing real estate transactions, blockchain could address many of the industry's current inefficiencies and issues.

However, it's important to note that the widespread adoption of blockchain in real estate faces several challenges. These include regulatory hurdles, the need for standardization across different blockchain platforms, and resistance from established players who benefit from the current system. Additionally, concerns about the energy consumption associated with some blockchain technologies need to be addressed.

Despite these challenges, I believe that blockchain technology will play a pivotal role in shaping the future of real estate transactions. Its potential to increase transparency, reduce fraud, lower costs, and improve efficiency aligns well with the needs of a modern, globalized real estate market. As the technology matures and these challenges are addressed, we expect to see increasing adoption of blockchain solutions in the real estate industry.

Deloitte's 2020 insights suggest that blockchain-based systems could democratize real estate by enabling fractional ownership, thus allowing more investors to access high-value properties with less capital upfront. The combination of these technologies on the Wizard platform could potentially set the standard for future real estate transactions globally. (Source: Deloitte, 2020)

By fully embracing blockchain technology, the Wizard platform has the potential to be at the forefront of this transformation, offering a glimpse into the future of real estate transactions. This future is more transparent, efficient, and accessible to all. (Source: Author's concluding thoughts based on the comprehensive analysis of blockchain potential in real estate)

How Long Until This Vision Is A Reality?

As we've explored the potential future of home sales throughout this book, a natural question arises: When will this vision become reality? Predicting the exact timeline for such a significant industry transformation is challenging. Still, we can make educated estimates based on current trends, technological advancements, and the pace of change in the real estate sector.

1. **Short-Term Developments (1-3 years):** In the immediate future, we'll likely see incremental improvements in existing technologies and their application to real estate. Virtual tours, AI-powered property recommendations, and

basic blockchain applications for record-keeping are already in use and will become more widespread. The Wizard platform, or similar innovative solutions, may gain traction in tech-forward markets. However, these platforms will likely coexist with traditional real estate models rather than entirely replacing them at this stage. (Source: Author's analysis based on current adoption rates of real estate technologies)

According to a study by the National Association of Realtors (NAR), 77% of homebuyers used online tools, such as property search engines and virtual tours, during their home search process. As these technologies improve, real estate platforms will increasingly integrate AI to provide more accurate, personalized suggestions. (Source: National Association of Realtors (NAR), 2023)

2. **Medium-term developments (3-7 years):** This period will likely see more substantial changes in real estate transactions. VR and AR for property viewing will become more sophisticated and widely adopted. Predictive analytics will play a more significant role in pricing and market analysis.

   I have predicted that within five years, at least 50% of initial property viewings in major urban markets will be conducted virtually. Blockchain-based smart contracts for real estate transactions will also become more common, particularly in tech-savvy regions. (Source: Author's prediction based on observed trends in technology adoption)

According to a 2023 report from PwC, 40% of real estate professionals are already using VR or AR for property tours, and this figure is expected to rise dramatically in the coming years. The National Association of Realtors (NAR) also highlighted that over 50% of potential buyers would prefer virtual tours, particularly in urban areas, indicating strong adoption of this technology for initial property viewings. By 2028, virtual property tours will likely dominate initial viewings in major metropolitan markets, aligning with the prediction that at least 50% of these viewings will be virtual (Source: PwC, 2023. NAR, 2023).

3. **Long-Term Developments (7-15 years):** This is when we might see the full realization of the vision outlined in this book. AI-driven platforms like the Wizard could become the primary means of conducting real estate transactions in many markets. Blockchain-based property records and transfers could become the norm rather than the exception. I believe that within 15 years, traditional real estate agents

will be replaced by AI-assisted platforms in most transactions, with human experts taking on more specialized advisory roles. (Source: Author's long-term prediction based on the potential trajectory of AI and blockchain technologies)

While AI platforms will dominate the transaction process, human real estate agents will not disappear entirely. Instead, they will evolve into specialized advisors, focusing on more complex decision-making areas, such as investment strategy, negotiation in high-value transactions, and dealing with unique or non-standard properties. As per Deloitte's 2023 real estate report, while AI is expected to handle the bulk of transactions, human expertise will still be valuable for certain aspects, particularly when it comes to legal nuances, emotional decision-making, and high-touch client service (Source: Deloitte, 2023).

4. **Factors influencing the timeline:** Several factors will influence how quickly this vision becomes a reality:
    - *Regulatory environment:* Changes in real estate regulations can either accelerate or hinder the adoption of new technologies. According to my notes, regulatory bodies often lag behind

technological advancements, which could slow the implementation of some innovations. (Source: Author's observation of regulatory trends in real estate)

- *Consumer acceptance:* The willingness of buyers and sellers to embrace new technologies will be crucial. Younger, tech-savvy generations entering the housing market may accelerate adoption. (Source: Author's analysis of generational trends in technology adoption)
- *Resistance from established players:* Traditional real estate companies and agents may resist changes threatening their business models. The strength and duration of this resistance will impact the speed of change. (Source: Author's observation of industry dynamics)
- *Technological advancements:* The pace of development in AI, VR/AR, and blockchain technologies will directly influence their application in real estate. (Source: Author's analysis of current technological trends)

5. **Regional Variations:** Adopting these new technologies and models will vary significantly by region. Tech-forward urban areas may see faster adoption, while rural

areas or markets with stricter regulations may lag behind. I have predicted that within a decade, we'll see a few "smart cities" where AI-driven, blockchain-based real estate transactions become the norm, serving as models for broader adoption. (Source: Author's prediction based on observed patterns of technology adoption in different markets)

Urban areas with higher tech penetration, such as San Francisco, New York, and London, are expected to be early adopters of technologies like AI-powered home recommendations, blockchain for transactions, and VR/AR for property tours. In fact, a McKinsey & Company report projects that by 2025, 75% of property transactions in major cities could incorporate some form of AI or blockchain technology (Source: McKinsey & Company, 2023). **Potential roadblocks:** Several challenges could slow down the realization of this vision:

- *Data privacy concerns:* As AI systems require vast amounts of personal data to function effectively, addressing privacy concerns will be crucial for widespread adoption. (Source: Author's analysis of current debates around data privacy)

- *Digital divide:* Ensuring equal access to these technologies across different socioeconomic groups will be a challenge that needs to be addressed. (Source: Author's observation of technology access disparities)
- *Cybersecurity:* As real estate transactions become increasingly digital, ensuring the security of these systems against cyber threats will be paramount. (Source: Author's analysis of cybersecurity challenges in digital transactions)
- ***Tipping point:*** I believe we're approaching a tipping point in the real estate industry. While change has been slow in the past, the convergence of AI, blockchain, and VR/AR technologies, combined with changing consumer expectations and consumer litigation, could lead to rapid transformation toward reaching a critical mass.

Today's consumers expect instant access to information, streamlined experiences, and personalized services across industries, including real estate. According to the National Association of Realtors (2022), over 80% of home buyers now begin their property search online, and this shift toward digital-first engagement is expected to continue driving the adoption of

AI-powered tools for property search and virtual home tours. (Source: National Association of Realtors, 2022)

I have predicted that this tipping point will occur within the next 5-7 years, after which the pace of change will accelerate dramatically. (Source: Author's prediction based on analysis of industry trends and technological advancements)

Blockchain has already begun to streamline property transactions by enabling secure, immutable records, reducing fraud, and eliminating the need for intermediaries. According to a Deloitte report (2022), blockchain's impact on real estate is predicted to cut transaction costs by 30% and reduce the closing period from weeks to mere days. These efficiencies are likely to increase as the technology becomes more widely adopted. (Source: Deloitte, 2022)

In conclusion, while the full realization of the vision outlined in this book may be 10-15 years away, we're likely to see significant changes in the real estate industry much sooner. The next decade will transition, with new models and technologies gradually replacing traditional practices.

The timeline will depend on technological advancements, regulatory changes, consumer acceptance, and industry dynamics. However, the change direction is clear: We're moving towards a more efficient, transparent, and technology-driven real estate market.

This transformation promises greater control, better information, and safer and more efficient consumer transactions. It represents both a challenge to adapt and an opportunity to create new value for the industry. Those who embrace these changes and innovate accordingly will be best positioned to thrive in the future of real estate.

As we stand on the brink of this transformation, it's an exciting time for the real estate industry. The vision we've explored in this book is more than just a distant possibility. An early version that solves the single-family transaction problems described in this book exists today. This vision is already a reality, but the prediction of when it is fully implemented is genuinely unknown. (Source: Author's concluding thoughts based on the comprehensive analysis presented in this chapter and throughout the book)

INDEX

Made in the USA
Monee, IL
04 November 2026

67384877R00164